BATTLE PIECES

The Civil War Poems

of

HERMAN MELVILLE

CASTLE BOOKS

NOTE: These poems were written in the immediate aftermath of the Civil War, and the text in this book is an exact facsimile of the original edition of 1866, published under the title *Battle-Pieces and Aspects of the War*. Some of the language used by Melville may be offensive to modern ears. The publishers remind the reader that some perspective and understanding of history is necessary in accounting for the author's language.

Published by Castle Books
a division of Book Sales, Inc.
114 Northfield Avenue
Edison, NJ 08837, USA

ISBN 0-7858-1282-2
Printed in the United States of America

THE BATTLE-PIECES

IN THIS VOLUME ARE DEDICATED

TO THE MEMORY OF THE

THREE HUNDRED THOUSAND

WHO IN THE WAR

FOR THE MAINTENANCE OF THE UNION

FELL DEVOTEDLY

UNDER THE FLAG OF THEIR FATHERS.

[WITH few exceptions, the Pieces in this volume originated in an impulse imparted by the fall of Richmond. They were composed without reference to collective arrangement, but, being brought together in review, naturally fall into the order assumed.

The events and incidents of the conflict — making up a whole, in varied amplitude, corresponding with the geographical area covered by the war — from these but a few themes have been taken, such as for any cause chanced to imprint themselves upon the mind.

The aspects which the strife as a memory assumes are as manifold as are the moods of involuntary meditation—moods variable, and at times widely at variance. Yielding instinctively, one after another, to feelings not inspired from any one source exclusively, and unmindful, without purposing to be, of consistency, I seem, in most of these verses, to have but placed a harp in a window, and noted the contrasted airs which wayward winds have played upon the strings.]

CONTENTS.

VERSES INSCRIPTIVE AND MEMORIAL.

The Portent.
(1859.)

Hanging from the beam,
   Slowly swaying (such the law),
Gaunt the shadow on your green,
   Shenandoah !
The cut is on the crown
(Lo, John Brown),
And the stabs shall heal no more.

Hidden in the cap
   Is the anguish none can draw;
So your future veils its face,
   Shenandoah !
But the streaming beard is shown
(Weird John Brown),
The meteor of the war.

Misgivings.

(1860.)

WHEN ocean-clouds over inland hills
    Sweep storming in late autumn brown,
And horror the sodden valley fills,
    And the spire falls crashing in the town,
I muse upon my country's ills—
The tempest bursting from the waste of Time
On the world's fairest hope linked with man's foulest
    crime.

Nature's dark side is heeded now—
    (Ah! optimist-cheer disheartened flown)—
A child may read the moody brow
    Of yon black mountain lone.
With shouts the torrents down the gorges go,
And storms are formed behind the storm we feel:
The hemlock shakes in the rafter, the oak in the driv-
    ing keel.

The Conflict of Convictions.[a]

(1860–1.)

On starry heights
  A bugle wails the long recall ;
Derision stirs the deep abyss,
  Heaven's ominous silence over all.
Return, return, O eager Hope,
  And face man's latter fall.
Events, they make the dreamers quail ;
Satan's old age is strong and hale,
A disciplined captain, gray in skill,
And Raphael a white enthusiast still ;
Dashed aims, at which Christ's martyrs pale,
Shall Mammon's slaves fulfill ?

> *(Dismantle the fort,*
> *Cut down the fleet—*
> *Battle no more shall be !*
> *While the fields for fight in æons to come*
> *Congeal beneath the sea.)*

The terrors of truth and dart of death
  To faith alike are vain ;
Though comets, gone a thousand years,
    Return again,
Patient she stands—she can no more—
And waits, nor heeds she waxes hoar.

(At a stony gate,
A statue of stone,
Weed overgrown—
Long 'twill wait !)

But God his former mind retains,
  Confirms his old decree ;
The generations are inured to pains,
  And strong Necessity
Surges, and heaps Time's strand with wrecks.
  The People spread like a weedy grass,
  The thing they will they bring to pass,
And prosper to the apoplex.
The rout it herds around the heart,
  The ghost is yielded in the gloom ;
Kings wag their heads—Now save thyself
  Who wouldst rebuild the world in bloom.

(Tide-mark
And top of the ages' strife,
Verge where they called the world to come,
The last advance of life—
Ha ha, the rust on the Iron Dome!)

Nay, but revere the hid event;
 In the cloud a sword is girded on,
I mark a twinkling in the tent
 Of Michael the warrior one.
Senior wisdom suits not now,
The light is on the youthful brow.

 (Ay, in caves the miner see:
 His forehead bears a blinking light;
 Darkness so he feebly braves—
 A meagre wight!)

But He who rules is old—is old;
Ah! faith is warm, but heaven with age is cold.

 (Ho ho, ho ho,
 The cloistered doubt
 Of olden times
 Is blurted out!)

The Ancient of Days forever is young,
　Forever the scheme of Nature thrives;
I know a wind in purpose strong—
　It spins *against* the way it drives.
What if the gulfs their slimed foundations bare?
So deep must the stones be hurled
Whereon the throes of ages rear
The final empire and the happier world.

　　　　(The poor old Past,
　　　　The Future's slave,
　　　　She drudged through pain and crime
　　　　To bring about the blissful Prime,
　　　　Then—perished. There's *a grave!)*

　Power unanointed may come—
Dominion (unsought by the free)
　And the' Iron Dome,
Stronger for stress and strain,
Fling her huge shadow athwart the main;
But the Founders' dream shall flee.
Age after age shall be
As age after age has been,
(From man's changeless heart their way they win);

And death be busy with all who strive—
Death, with silent negative.

YEA AND NAY—
EACH HATH HIS SAY;
BUT GOD HE KEEPS THE MIDDLE WAY.
NONE WAS BY
WHEN HE SPREAD THE SKY;
WISDOM IS VAIN, AND PROPHESY.

Apathy and Enthusiasm.

(1860–1.)

I.

O THE clammy cold November,
    And the winter white and dead,
And the terror dumb with stupor,
    And the sky a sheet of lead;
And events that came resounding
    With the cry that *All was lost*,
Like the thunder-cracks of massy ice
    In intensity of frost—
Bursting one upon another
    Through the horror of the calm.
    The paralysis of arm
In the anguish of the heart;
And the hollowness and dearth.
    The appealings of the mother
    To brother and to brother
Not in hatred so to part—
And the fissure in the hearth

Growing momently more wide.
Then the glances 'tween the Fates,
   And the doubt on every side,
And the patience under gloom
In the stoniness that waits
The finality of doom.

II.

So the winter died despairing,
   And the weary weeks of Lent ;
And the ice-bound rivers melted,
   And the tomb of Faith was rent.
O, the rising of the People
   Came with springing of the grass,
They rebounded from dejection
   After Easter came to pass.
And the young were all elation
   Hearing Sumter's cannon roar,
And they thought how tame the Nation
   In the age that went before.
And Michael seemed gigantical,
   The Arch-fiend but a dwarf;
And at the towers of Erebus
   Our striplings flung the scoff.
But the elders with foreboding
   Mourned the days forever o'er,

And recalled the forest proverb,
The Iroquois' old saw:
*Grief to every graybeard
When young Indians lead the war.*

The March into Virginia,

Ending in the First Manassas.

(July, 1861.)

Did all the lets and bars appear
   To every just or larger end,
Whence should come the trust and cheer?
   Youth must its ignorant impulse lend—
Age finds place in the rear.
   All wars are boyish, and are fought by boys,
The champions and enthusiasts of the state :
   Turbid ardors and vain joys
     Not barrenly abate—
   Stimulants to the power mature,
     Preparatives of fate.

Who here forecasteth the event?
What heart but spurns at precedent
And warnings of the wise,
Contemned foreclosures of surprise?

The banners play, the bugles call,
The air is blue and prodigal.
　No berrying party, pleasure-wooed,
No picnic party in the May,
Ever went less loth than they
　Into that leafy neighborhood.
In Bacchic glee they file toward Fate,
Moloch's uninitiate ;
Expectancy, and glad surmise
Of battle's unknown mysteries.
All they feel is this : 'tis glory,
A rapture sharp, though transitory,
Yet lasting in belaureled story.
So they gayly go to fight,
Chatting left and laughing right.

But some who this blithe mood present,
　As on in lightsome files they fare,
Shall die experienced ere three days are spent—
　Perish, enlightened by the vollied glare ;
Or shame survive, and, like to adamant,
　The throe of Second Manassas share.

Lyon.

Battle of Springfield, Missouri.

(August, 1861.)

Some hearts there are of deeper sort,
　　Prophetic, sad,
Which yet for cause are trebly clad;
　　Known death they fly on:
This wizard-heart and heart-of-oak had Lyon.

"They are more than twenty thousand strong,
　　We less than five,
Too few with such a host to strive."
　　"Such counsel, fie on!
'Tis battle, or 'tis shame;" and firm stood Lyon.

"For help at need in vain we wait—
　　Retreat or fight:
Retreat the foe would take for flight,
　　And each proud scion
Feel more elate; the end must come," said Lyon.

By candlelight he wrote the will,
    And left his all
To Her for whom 'twas not enough to fall;
    Loud neighed Orion
Without the tent; drums beat; we marched with Lyon.

The night-tramp done, we spied the Vale
    With guard-fires lit;
Day broke, but trooping clouds made gloom of it:
    "A field to die on,"
Presaged in his unfaltering heart, brave Lyon.

We fought on the grass, we bled in the corn—
    Fate seemed malign;
His horse the Leader led along the line—
    Star-browed Orion;
Bitterly fearless, he rallied us there, brave Lyon.

There came a sound like the slitting of air
    By a swift sharp sword—
A rush of the sound; and the sleek chest broad
    Of black Orion
Heaved, and was fixed; the dead mane waved toward Lyon.

B

"General, you're hurt—this sleet of balls!"
  He seemed half spent;
With moody and bloody brow, he lowly bent:
  "The field to die on;
But not—not yet; the day is long," breathed Lyon.

For a time becharmed there fell a lull
  In the heart of the fight;
The tree-tops nod, the slain sleep light;
  Warm noon-winds sigh on,
And thoughts which he never spake had Lyon.

Texans and Indians trim for a charge:
  "Stand ready, men!
Let them come close, right up, and then
  After the lead, the iron;
Fire, and charge back!" So strength returned to Lyon.

The Iowa men who held the van,
  Half drilled, were new
To battle: "Some one lead us, then we'll do,"
  Said Corporal Tryon:
"Men! *I* will lead," and a light glared in Lyon.

On they came : they yelped, and fired ;
  His spirit sped ;
We leveled right in, and the half-breeds fled,
  Nor stayed the iron,
Nor captured the crimson corse of Lyon.

This seer foresaw his soldier-doom,
  Yet willed the fight.
He never turned ; his only flight
  Was up to Zion,
Where prophets now and armies greet brave Lyon.

Ball's Bluff.

A Reverie.

(OCTOBER, 1861.)

ONE noonday, at my window in the town,
   I saw a sight—saddest that eyes can see—
Young soldiers marching lustily
      Unto the wars,
With fifes, and flags in mottoed pageantry;
   While all the porches, walks, and doors
Were rich with ladies cheering royally.

They moved like Juny morning on the wave,
   Their hearts were fresh as clover in its prime
   (It was the breezy summer time),
      Life throbbed so strong,
How should they dream that Death in a rosy clime
   Would come to thin their shining throng?
Youth feels immortal, like the gods sublime.

Weeks passed ; and at my window, leaving bed,
  By night I mused, of easeful sleep bereft,
    On those brave boys (Ah War ! thy theft) ;
        Some marching feet
Found pause at last by cliffs Potomac cleft ;
    Wakeful I mused, while in the street
Far footfalls died away till none were left.

Dupont's Round Fight.

(November, 1861.)

In time and measure perfect moves
  All Art whose aim is sure;
Evolving rhyme and stars divine
  Have rules, and they endure.

Nor less the Fleet that warred for Right,
  And, warring so, prevailed,
In geometric beauty curved,
  And in an orbit sailed.

The rebel at Port Royal felt
  The Unity overawe,
And rued the spell. A type was here,
  And victory of Law.

The Stone Fleet:[b]

An Old Sailor's Lament.

(DECEMBER, 1861.)

I HAVE a feeling for those ships,
   Each worn and ancient one,
With great bluff bows, and broad in the beam.
   Ay, it was unkindly done.
         But so they serve the Obsolete—
         Even so, Stone Fleet!

You'll say I'm doting; do but think
   I scudded round the Horn in one—
The Tenedos, a glorious
   Good old craft as ever run—
         Sunk (how all unmeet!)
         With the Old Stone Fleet.

An India ship of fame was she,
   Spices and shawls and fans she bore;

A whaler when her wrinkles came—
  Turned off! till, spent and poor,
        Her bones were sold (escheat)!
        Ah! Stone Fleet.

Four were erst patrician keels
  (Names attest what families be),
The Kensington, and Richmond too,
  Leonidas, and Lee:
        But now they have their seat
        With the Old Stone Fleet.

To scuttle them—a pirate deed—
  Sack them, and dismast;
They sunk so slow, they died so hard,
  But gurgling dropped at last.
        Their ghosts in gales repeat
        Woe's us, Stone Fleet!

And all for naught. The waters pass—
  Currents will have their way;
Nature is nobody's ally; 'tis well;
  The harbor is bettered—will stay.
        A failure, and complete,
        Was your Old Stone Fleet.

Donelson.

(February, 1862.)

THE bitter cup
  Of that hard countermand
Which gave the Envoys up,
Still was wormwood in the mouth,
  And clouds involved the land,
When, pelted by sleet in the icy street,
  About the bulletin-board a band
Of eager, anxious people met,
And every wakeful heart was set
On latest news from West or South.
"No seeing here," cries one—"don't crowd"—
"You tall man, pray you, read aloud."

IMPORTANT.

    We learn that General Grant,
  Marching from Henry overland,
And joined by a force up the Cumberland sent
  (Some thirty thousand the command),

B 2

On Wednesday a good position won—
Began the siege of Donelson.

This stronghold crowns a river-bluff,
　A good broad mile of leveled top;
Inland the ground rolls off
　Deep-gorged, and rocky, and broken up—
A wilderness of trees and brush.
　The spaded summit shows the roods
Of fixed intrenchments in their hush;
　Breast-works and rifle-pits in woods
Perplex the base.—
　　　　　　　The welcome weather
　Is clear and mild; 'tis much like May.
The ancient boughs that lace together
Along the stream, and hang far forth,
　Strange with green mistletoe, betray
A dreamy contrast to the North.

Our troops are full of spirits—say
　The siege won't prove a creeping one.
They purpose not the lingering stay
Of old beleaguerers; not that way;
　But, full of vim *from Western prairies won,*
　They'll make, ere long, a dash at Donelson.

Washed by the storm till the paper grew
Every shade of a streaky blue,
That bulletin stood. The next day brought
A second.

LATER FROM THE FORT.

Grant's investment is complete—
A semicircular one.
Both wings the Cumberland's margin meet,
Then, backward curving, clasp the rebel seat.
On Wednesday this good work was done;
But of the doers some lie prone.
Each wood, each hill, each glen was fought for;
The bold inclosing line we wrought for
Flamed with sharpshooters. Each cliff cost
A limb or life. But back we forced
Reserves and all; made good our hold;
And so we rest.

Events unfold.

On Thursday added ground was won,
A long bold steep: we near the Den.
Later the foe came shouting down
In sortie, which was quelled; and then
We stormed them on their left.
A chilly change in the afternoon;

The sky, late clear, is now bereft
Of sun.   Last night the ground froze hard—
Rings to the enemy as they run
Within their works.   A ramrod bites
The lip it meets.   The cold incites
To swinging of arms with brisk rebound.
Smart blows 'gainst lusty chests resound.

Along the outer line we ward
    A crackle of skirmishing goes on.
Our lads creep round on hand and knee,
        They fight from behind each trunk and stone;
        And sometimes, flying for refuge, one
Finds 'tis an enemy shares the tree.
Some scores are maimed by boughs shot off
        In the glades by the Fort's big gun.
        We mourn the loss of Colonel Morrison,
        Killed while cheering his regiment on.
Their far sharpshooters try our stuff;
And ours return them puff for puff:
'Tis diamond-cutting-diamond work.
    Woe on the rebel cannoneer
Who shows his head.   Our fellows lurk
    Like Indians that waylay the deer
By the wild salt-spring.—The sky is dun,
Foredooming the fall of Donelson.

Stern weather is all unwonted here.
   The people of the country own
We brought it.   Yea, the earnest North
Has elementally issued forth
   To storm this Donelson.

FURTHER.

            A yelling rout
Of ragamuffins broke profuse
   To-day from out the Fort.
   Sole uniform they wore, a sort
Of patch, or white badge (as you choose)
   Upon the arm.   But leading these,
Or mingling, were men of face
And bearing of patrician race,
Splendid in courage and gold lace—
   The officers.   Before the breeze
Made by their charge, down went our line;
But, rallying, charged back in force,
And broke the sally; yet with loss.
This on the left; upon the right
Meanwhile there was an answering fight;
   Assailants and assailed reversed.
The charge too upward, and not down—
Up a steep ridge-side, toward its crown,
   A strong redoubt.   But they who first

Gained the fort's base, and marked the trees
Felled, heaped in horned perplexities,
   And shagged with brush; and swarming there
Fierce wasps whose sting was present death—
They faltered, drawing bated breath,
   And felt it was in vain to dare;
Yet still, perforce, returned the ball,
Firing into the tangled wall
Till ordered to come down. They came;
But left some comrades in their fame,
Red on the ridge in icy wreath
And hanging gardens of cold Death.
   But not quite unavenged these fell;
Our ranks once out of range, a blast
   Of shrapnel and quick shell
Burst on the rebel horde, still massed,
   Scattering them pell-mell.
      (This fighting—judging what we read—
      Both charge and countercharge,
      Would seem but Thursday's told at large,
      Before in brief reported.—Ed.)
Night closed in about the Den
   Murky and lowering. Ere long, chill rains.
A night not soon to be forgot,
   Reviving old rheumatic pains
And longings for a cot.

No blankets, overcoats, or tents.
Coats thrown aside on the warm march here—
We looked not then for changeful cheer;
Tents, coats, and blankets too much care.
  No fires; a fire a mark presents;
  Near by, the trees show bullet-dents.
Rations were eaten cold and raw.
    The men well soaked, came snow; and more—
A midnight sally. Small sleeping done—
      But such is war;
No matter, we'll have Fort Donelson.

        "Ugh! ugh!
'Twill drag along—drag along,"
Growled a cross patriot in the throng,
His battered umbrella like an ambulance-cover
Riddled with bullet-holes, spattered all over.
"Hurrah for Grant!" cried a stripling shrill;
Three urchins joined him with a will,
And some of taller stature cheered.
Meantime a Copperhead passed; he sneered.
  "Win or lose," he pausing said,
"Caps fly the same; all boys, mere boys;
Any thing to make a noise.
  Like to see the list of the dead;

These '*craven Southerners*' hold out;
Ay, ay, they'll give you many a bout."
  "We'll beat in the end, sir,"
Firmly said one in staid rebuke,
A solid merchant, square and stout.
  "And do you think it? that way tend, sir?"
Asked the lean Copperhead, with a look
Of splenetic pity. "Yes, I do."
His yellow death's head the croaker shook:
"The country's ruined, that I know."
A shower of broken ice and snow,
  In lieu of words, confuted him;
They saw him hustled round the corner go,
  And each by-stander said—Well suited him.

Next day another crowd was seen
In the dark weather's sleety spleen.
Bald-headed to the storm came out
A man, who, 'mid a joyous shout,
Silently posted this brief sheet:

  GLORIOUS VICTORY OF THE FLEET!

  FRIDAY'S GREAT EVENT!

  THE ENEMY'S WATER-BATTERIES BEAT!

WE SILENCED EVERY GUN!

THE OLD COMMODORE'S COMPLIMENTS SENT
PLUMP INTO DONELSON!

"Well, well, go on!" exclaimed the crowd
To him who thus much read aloud.
"That's all," he said. "What! nothing more?"
"Enough for a cheer, though—hip, hurrah!
"But here's old Baldy come again—
"More news!"—And now a different strain.

(Our own reporter a dispatch compiles,
  As best he may, from varied sources.)

Large re-enforcements have arrived—
  Munitions, men, and horses—
For Grant, and all debarked, with stores.

  The enemy's field-works extend six miles—
The gate still hid; so well contrived.

Yesterday stung us; frozen shores
  Snow-clad, and through the drear defiles

And over the desolate ridges blew
A Lapland wind.

          The main affair
Was a good two hours' steady fight
Between our gun-boats and the Fort.

   The Louisville's wheel was smashed outright.
A hundred-and-twenty-eight-pound ball
Came planet-like through a starboard port,
Killing three men, and wounding all
The rest of that gun's crew,
(The captain of the gun was cut in two);
Then splintering and ripping went—
Nothing could be its continent.

   In the narrow stream the Louisville,
Unhelmed, grew lawless; swung around,

     And would have thumped and drifted, till
All the fleet was driven aground,
But for the timely order to retire.

Some damage from our fire, 'tis thought,
Was done the water-batteries of the Fort.

Little else took place that day,
    Except the field artillery in line
Would now and then—for love, they say—
    Exchange a valentine.

The old sharpshooting going on.
Some plan afoot as yet unknown;
So Friday closed round Donelson.

LATER.

      Great suffering through the night—
A stinging ·one. Our heedless boys
  Were nipped like blossoms. Some dozen
  Hapless wounded men were frozen.
During day being struck down out of sight,
And help-cries drowned in roaring noise,
They were left just where the skirmish shifted—
Left in dense underbrush snow-drifted.
Some, seeking to crawl in crippled plight,
So stiffened—perished.

                Yet in spite
Of pangs for these, no heart is lost.
Hungry, and clothing stiff with frost,
Our men declare a nearing sun
Shall see the fall of Donelson.
  And this they say, yet not disown
The dark redoubts round Donelson,
  And ice-glazed corpses, each a stone—
    A sacrifice to Donelson;
They swear it, and swerve not, gazing on
A flag, deemed black, flying from Donelson.

Some of the wounded in the wood
Were cared for by the foe last night,
Though he could do them little needed good,
Himself being all in shivering plight.
The rebel is wrong, but human yet;
He's got a heart, and thrusts a bayonet.
He gives us battle with wondrous will—
This bluff's a perverted Bunker Hill.

The stillness stealing through the throng
The silent thought and dismal fear revealed ;
  They turned and went,
  Musing on right and wrong
  And mysteries dimly sealed—
Breasting the storm in daring discontent ;
The storm, whose black flag showed in heaven,
As if to say no quarter there was given
  To wounded men in wood,
  Or true hearts yearning for the good—
All fatherless seemed the human soul.
But next day brought a bitterer bowl—
  On the bulletin-board this stood :

Saturday morning at 3 A.M.
A stir within the Fort betrayed
That the rebels were getting under arms;
Some plot these early birds had laid.

But a lancing sleet cut him who stared
Into the storm.   After some vague alarms,
Which left our lads unscared,
Out sallied the enemy at dim of dawn,
    With cavalry and artillery, and went
        In fury at our environment.
Under cover of shot and shell
    Three columns of infantry rolled on,
    Vomited out of Donelson—
Rolled down the slopes like rivers of hell,
    Surged at our line, and swelled and poured
Like breaking surf.   But unsubmerged
    Our men stood up, except where roared
The enemy through one gap.   We urged
Our all of manhood to the stress,
But still showed shattered in our desperateness.
        Back set the tide,
But soon afresh rolled in;
    And so it swayed from side to side—
Far batteries joining in the din,
Though sharing in another fray—
    Till all became an Indian fight,
Intricate, dusky, stretching far away,
Yet not without spontaneous plan
    However tangled showed the plight:
Duels all over 'tween man and man,

Duels on cliff-side, and down in ravine,
  Duels at long range, and bone to bone;
Duels every where flitting and half unseen.
  Only by courage good as their own,
And strength outlasting theirs,
  Did our boys at last drive the rebels off.
Yet they went not back to their distant lairs
  In strong-hold, but loud in scoff
Maintained themselves on conquered ground—
Uplands; built works, or stalked around.
Our right wing bore this onset. Noon
Brought calm to Donelson.

The reader ceased; the storm beat hard;
  'Twas day, but the office-gas was lit;
  Nature retained her sulking-fit,
    In her hand the shard.
Flitting faces took the hue
Of that washed bulletin-board in view,
And seemed to bear the public grief
As private, and uncertain of relief;
Yea, many an earnest heart was won,
  As broodingly he plodded on,
To find in himself some bitter thing,
Some hardness in his lot as harrowing
    As Donelson.

That night the board stood barren there,
　　Oft eyed by wistful people passing,
　　Who nothing saw but the rain-beads chasing
Each other down the wafered square,
As down some storm-beat grave-yard stone.
But next day showed—

　　　　　　MORE NEWS LAST NIGHT.

　　STORY OF SATURDAY AFTERNOON.

　　VICISSITUDES OF THE WAR.

　　The damaged gun-boats can't wage fight
For days; so says the Commodore.
Thus no diversion can be had.
Under a sunless sky of lead
　　Our grim-faced boys in blackened plight
Gaze toward the ground they held before,
And then on Grant. He marks their mood,
And hails it, and will turn the same to good.
Spite all that they have undergone,
Their desperate hearts are set upon
This winter fort, this stubborn fort,
This castle of the last resort,
　　　　This Donelson.

1 P.M.

> An order given
> Requires withdrawal from the front
> Of regiments that bore the brunt
> Of morning's fray.   Their ranks all riven
> Are being replaced by fresh, strong men.
> Great vigilance in the foeman's Den;
> He snuffs the stormers.   Need it is
> That for that fell assault of his,
> That rout inflicted, and self-scorn—
> Immoderate in noble natures, torn
> By sense of being through slackness overborne—
> The rebel be given a quick return:
> The kindest face looks now half stern.
> Balked of their prey in airs that freeze,
> Some fierce ones glare like savages.
> And yet, and yet, strange moments are—
> Well—blood, and tears, and anguished War!
> The morning's battle-ground is seen
> In lifted glades, like meadows rare;
> The blood-drops on the snow-crust there
> Like clover in the white-weed show—
> Flushed fields of death, that call again—
> Call to our men, and not in vain,
> For that way must the stormers go.

3 *P.M.*

The work begins.
Light drifts of men thrown forward, fade
　In skirmish-line along the slope,
Where some dislodgments must be made
　Ere the stormer with the strong-hold cope.

Lew Wallace, moving to retake
The heights late lost—
　　　　　(Herewith a break.
Storms at the West derange the wires.
Doubtless, ere morning, we shall hear
The end; we look for news to cheer—
　Let Hope fan all her fires.)

Next day in large bold hand was seen
The closing bulletin :

Victory !
　　　Our troops have retrieved the day
By one grand surge along the line;
The spirit that urged them was divine.
　The first works flooded, naught could stay
The stormers : on ! still on !
Bayonets for Donelson !

C

Over the ground that morning lost
Rolled the blue billows, tempest-tossed,
   Following a hat on the point of a sword.
Spite shell and round-shot, grape and canister,
Up they climbed without rail or banister—
   Up the steep hill-sides long and broad,
Driving the rebel deep within his works.
'Tis nightfall; not an enemy lurks
   In sight. The chafing men
     Fret for more fight:
" To-night, to-night let us take the Den!"
But night is treacherous, Grant is wary;
Of brave blood be a little chary.
Patience! the Fort is good as won;
To-morrow, and into Donelson.

LATER AND LAST.

THE FORT IS OURS.

   A flag came out at early morn
Bringing surrender. From their towers
   Floats out the banner late their scorn.
In Dover, hut and house are full
   Of rebels dead or dying.
   The National flag is flying
From the crammed court-house pinnacle.

Great boat-loads of our wounded go
To-day to Nashville. The sleet-winds blow;
But all is right: the fight is won,
The winter-fight for Donelson.
   Hurrah!
The spell of old defeat is broke,
 The habit of victory begun;
Grant strikes the war's first sounding stroke
  At Donelson.

For lists of killed and wounded, see
The morrow's dispatch: to-day 'tis victory.

The man who read this to the crowd
 Shouted as the end he gained;
 And though the unflagging tempest rained,
  They answered him aloud.
And hand grasped hand, and glances met
In happy triumph; eyes grew wet.
O, to the punches brewed that night
Went little water. Windows bright
Beamed rosy on the sleet without,
And from the deep street came the frequent shout;
While some in prayer, as these in glee,
Blessed heaven for the winter-victory.

But others were who wakeful laid
  In midnight beds, and early rose,
  And, feverish in the foggy snows,
Snatched the damp paper—wife and maid.
  The death-list like a river flows
    Down the pale sheet,
And there the whelming waters meet.

  Ah God! may Time with happy haste
  Bring wail and triumph to a waste,
    And war be done ;
  The battle flag-staff fall athwart
  The curs'd ravine, and wither ; naught
    Be left of trench or gun ;
  The bastion, let it ebb away,
  Washed with the river bed ; and Day
    In vain seek Donelson.

The Cumberland.

(MARCH, 1862.)

SOME names there are of telling sound,
  Whose voweled syllables free
Are pledge that they shall ever live renowned;
    Such seems to be
A Frigate's name (by present glory spanned)—
    The Cumberland.

      Sounding name as ere was sung,
      Flowing, rolling on the tongue—
      Cumberland! Cumberland!

She warred and sunk.   There's no denying
  That she was ended—quelled;
And yet her flag above her fate is flying,
    As when it swelled
Unswallowed by the swallowing sea: so grand—
    The Cumberland.

Goodly name as ere was sung,
Roundly rolling on the tongue—
Cumberland ! Cumberland !

What need to tell how she was fought—
The sinking flaming gun—
The gunner leaping out the port—
Washed back, undone !
Her dead unconquerably manned
The Cumberland.

Noble name as ere was sung,
Slowly roll it on the tongue—
Cumberland ! Cumberland !

Long as hearts shall share the flame
Which burned in that brave crew,
Her fame shall live—outlive the victor's name ;
For this is due.
Your flag and flag-staff shall in story stand—
Cumberland !

Sounding name as ere was sung,
Long they'll roll it on the tongue—
Cumberland ! Cumberland !

In the Turret.

(MARCH, 1862.)

———

YOUR honest heart of duty, Worden,
  So helped you that in fame you dwell;
You bore the first iron battle's burden
  Sealed as in a diving-bell.
Alcides, groping into haunted hell
To bring forth King Admetus' bride,
Braved naught more vaguely direful and untried.
  What poet shall uplift his charm,
Bold Sailor, to your height of daring,
  And interblend therewith the calm,
And build a goodly style upon your bearing.

Escaped the gale of outer ocean—
  Cribbed in a craft which like a log
Was washed by every billow's motion—
  By night you heard of Og
The huge; nor felt your courage clog

At tokens of his onset grim :
You marked the sunk ship's flag-staff slim,
   Lit by her burning sister's heart ;
You marked, and mused : " Day brings the trial :
   Then be it proved if I have part
With men whose manhood never took denial."

A prayer went up—a champion's. Morning
   Beheld you in the Turret walled
By adamant, where a spirit forewarning
   And all-deriding called :
" Man, darest thou—desperate, unappalled—
Be first to lock thee in the armored tower ?
I have thee now ; and what the battle-hour
   To me shall bring—heed well—thou'lt share ;
This plot-work, planned to be the foeman's terror,
   To thee may prove a goblin-snare ;
Its very strength and cunning—monstrous error !"

" Stand up, my heart ; be strong ; what matter
   If here thou seest thy welded tomb ?
And let huge Og with thunders batter—
   Duty be still my doom,
Though drowning come in liquid gloom ;

First duty, duty next, and duty last;
Ay, Turret, rivet me here to duty fast!"—
  So nerved, you fought, wisely and well;
And live, twice live in life and story;
  But over your Monitor dirges swell,
In wind and wave that keep the rites of glory.

C 2

The Temeraire.^c

(Supposed to have been suggested to an Englishman of the old order by the fight of the Monitor and Merrimac.)

THE gloomy hulls, in armor grim,
  Like clouds o'er moors have met,
And prove that oak, and iron, and man
  Are tough in fibre yet.

But Splendors wane.   The sea-fight yields
  No front of old display ;
The garniture, emblazonment,
  And heraldry all decay.

Towering afar in parting light,
  The fleets like Albion's forelands shine—
The full-sailed fleets, the shrouded show
  Of Ships-of-the-Line.

The fighting Temeraire,
  Built of a thousand trees,
Lunging out her lightnings,
  And beetling o'er the seas—
O Ship, how brave and fair,
  That fought so oft and well,
On open decks you manned the gun
    Armorial.[d]
What cheerings did you share,
  Impulsive in the van,
When down upon leagued France and Spain
  We English ran—
The freshet at your bowsprit
  Like the foam upon the can.
Bickering, your colors
  Licked up the Spanish air,
You flapped with flames of battle-flags—
  Your challenge, Temeraire!
The rear ones of our fleet
  They yearned to share your place,
Still vying with the Victory
  Throughout that earnest race—
The Victory, whose Admiral,
  With orders nobly won,
Shone in the globe of the battle glow—
  The angel in that sun.

Parallel in story,
  Lo, the stately pair,
As late in grapple ranging,
  The foe between them there—
When four great hulls lay tiered,
And the fiery tempest cleared,
And your prizes twain appeared,
    Temeraire!

But Trafalgar' is over now,
  The quarter-deck undone;
The carved and castled navies fire
  Their evening-gun.
O, Titan Temeraire,
  Your stern-lights fade away;
Your bulwarks to the years must yield,
  And heart-of-oak decay.
A pigmy steam-tug tows you,
  Gigantic, to the shore—
Dismantled of your guns and spars,
  And sweeping wings of war.
The rivets clinch the iron-clads,
  Men learn a deadlier lore;
But Fame has nailed your battle-flags—
  Your ghost it sails before:
O, the navies old and oaken,
  O, the Temeraire no more!

A Utilitarian View of the Monitor's Fight.

PLAIN be the phrase, yet apt the verse,
　More ponderous than nimble;
For since grimed War here laid aside
His Orient pomp, 'twould ill befit
　　Overmuch to ply
　The rhyme's barbaric cymbal.

Hail to victory without the gaud
　Of glory; zeal that needs no fans
Of banners; plain mechanic power
Plied cogently in War now placed—
　　Where War belongs—
　Among the trades and artisans.

Yet this was battle, and intense—
　Beyond the strife of fleets heroic;
Deadlier, closer, calm 'mid storm;

No passion; all went on by crank,
    Pivot, and screw,
  And calculations of caloric.

Needless to dwell; the story's known.
  The ringing of those plates on plates
Still ringeth round the world—
The clangor of that blacksmiths' fray.
    The anvil-din
  Resounds this message from the Fates:

War shall yet be, and to the end;
  But war-paint shows the streaks of weather;
War yet shall be, but warriors
Are now but operatives; War's made
    Less grand than Peace,
  And a singe runs through lace and feather.

Shiloh.

A Requiem.

(APRIL, 1862.)

SKIMMING lightly, wheeling still,
  The swallows fly low
Over the field in clouded days,
  The forest-field of Shiloh—
Over the field where April rain
Solaced the parched ones stretched in pain
Through the pause of night
That followed the Sunday fight
  Around the church of Shiloh—
The church so lone, the log-built one,
That echoed to many a parting groan
    And natural prayer
  Of dying foemen mingled there—
Foemen at morn, but friends at eve—
  Fame or country least their care:
(What like a bullet can undeceive!)
  But now they lie low,
While over them the swallows skim,
  And all is hushed at Shiloh.

The Battle for the Mississippi.

(APRIL, 1862.)

WHEN Israel camped by Migdol hoar,
  Down at her feet her shawm she threw,
But Moses sung and timbrels rung
  For Pharaoh's stranded crew.
So God appears in apt events—
  The Lord is a man of war!
So the strong wing to the muse is given
      In victory's roar.

Deep be the ode that hymns the fleet—
  The fight by night—the fray
Which bore our Flag against the powerful stream,
  And led it up to day.
Dully through din of larger strife
  Shall bay that warring gun;
But none the less to us who live
  It peals—an echoing one.

The shock of ships, the jar of walls,
  The rush through thick and thin—
The flaring fire-rafts, glare and gloom—
  Eddies, and shells that spin—
The boom-chain burst, the hulks dislodged,
  The jam of gun-boats driven,
Or fired, or sunk—made up a war
  Like Michael's waged with leven.

The manned Varuna stemmed and quelled
  The odds which hard beset;
The oaken flag-ship, half ablaze,
  Passed on and thundered yet;
While foundering, gloomed in grimy flame,
  The Ram Manassas—hark the yell!—
Plunged, and was gone; in joy or fright,
  The River gave a startled swell.

They fought through lurid dark till dawn;
  The war-smoke rolled away
With clouds of night, and showed the fleet
  In scarred yet firm array,
Above the forts, above the drift
  Of wrecks which strife had made;

And Farragut sailed up to the town
And anchored—sheathed the blade.

The moody broadsides, brooding deep,
  Hold the lewd mob at bay,
While o'er the armed decks' solemn aisles
  The meek church-pennons play;
By shotted guns the sailors stand,
  With foreheads bound or bare;
The captains and the conquering crews
  Humble their pride in prayer.

They pray; and after victory, prayer
  Is meet for men who mourn their slain;
The living shall unmoor and sail,
  But Death's dark anchor secret deeps detain.
Yet Glory slants her shaft of rays
  Far through the undisturbed abyss;
There must be other, nobler worlds for them
  Who nobly yield their lives in this.

Malvern Hill.

(JULY, 1862.)

YE elms that wave on Malvern Hill
  In prime of morn and May,
Recall ye how McClellan's men
    Here stood at bay?
While deep within 'yon forest dim
    Our rigid comrades lay—
Some with the cartridge in their mouth,
Others with fixed arms lifted South—
    Invoking so
The cypress glades? Ah wilds of woe!

The spires of Richmond, late beheld
  Through rifts in musket-haze,
Were closed from view in clouds of dust
    On leaf-walled ways,
Where streamed our wagons in caravan;
  And the Seven Nights and Days

Of march and fast, retreat and fight,
Pinched our grimed faces to ghastly plight—
　　Does the elm wood
Recall the haggard beards of blood?

The battle-smoked flag, with stars eclipsed,
　We followed (it never fell!)—
In silence husbanded our strength—
　　Received their yell;
Till on this slope we patient turned
　With cannon ordered well;
Reverse we proved was not defeat;
But ah, the sod what thousands meet!—
　　Does Malvern Wood
Bethink itself, and muse and brood?

We elms of Malvern Hill
*　Remember every thing;*
But sap the twig will fill:
Wag the world how it will,
*　Leaves must be green in Spring.*

The Victor of Antietam.[e]
(1862.)

WHEN tempest winnowed grain from bran,
And men were looking for a man,
Authority called you to the van,
        McClellan :
Along the line the plaudit ran,
As later when Antietam's cheers began.

Through storm-cloud and eclipse must move
Each Cause and Man, dear to the stars and Jove ;
Nor always can the wisest tell
Deferred fulfillment from the hopeless knell—
The struggler from the floundering ne'er-do-well.
A pall-cloth on the Seven Days fell,
        McClellan—
Unprosperously heroical !
Who could Antietam's wreath foretell ?

Authority called you ; then, in mist
And loom of jeopardy—dismissed.
But staring peril soon appalled ;
You, the Discarded, she recalled—
Recalled you, nor endured delay ;
And forth you rode upon a blasted way,
Arrayed Pope's rout, and routed Lee's array,
   McClellan :
Your tent was choked with captured flags that day,
   McClellan.
Antietam was a telling fray.

Recalled you ; and she heard your drum
Advancing through the ghastly gloom.
You manned the wall, you propped the Dome,
You stormed the powerful stormer home,
   McClellan :
Antietam's cannon long shall boom.

At Alexandria, left alone,
   McClellan—
Your veterans sent from you, and thrown
To fields and fortunes all unknown—
What thoughts were yours, revealed to none,

While faithful still you labored on—
Hearing the far Manassas gun!
        McClellan,
Only Antietam could atone.

You fought in the front (an evil day,
        McClellan)—
The fore-front of the first assay;
The Cause went sounding, groped its way;
The leadsmen quarrelled in the bay;
Quills thwarted swords; divided sway;
The rebel flushed in his lusty May:
You did your best, as in you lay,
        McClellan.
Antietam's sun-burst sheds a ray.

Your medalled soldiers love you well,
        McClellan:
Name your name, their true hearts swell;
With you they shook dread Stonewall's spell,[f]
With you they braved the blended yell
Of rebel and maligner fell;
With you in shame or fame they dwell,
        McClellan:
Antietam-braves a brave can tell.

And when your comrades (now so few,
            McClellan—
Such ravage in deep files they rue)
Meet round the board, and sadly view
The empty places ; tribute due
They render to the dead—and you !
Absent and silent o'er the blue ;
The one-armed lift the wine to *you*,
            McClellan,
And great Antietam's cheers renew.

Battle of Stone River, Tennessee.
A View from Oxford Cloisters.
(January, 1863.)

───────────

With Tewksbury and Barnet heath
   In days to come the field shall blend,
The story dim and date obscure;
   In legend all shall end.
Even now, involved in forest shade
   A Druid-dream the strife appears,
The fray of yesterday assumes
   The haziness of years.
      In North and South still beats the vein
      Of Yorkist and Lancastrian.

Our rival Roses warred for Sway—
   For Sway, but named the name of Right;
And Passion, scorning pain and death,
   Lent sacred fervor to the fight.
Each lifted up a broidered cross,
   While crossing blades profaned the sign;

D

Monks blessed the fratricidal lance,
   And sisters scarfs could twine.
      Do North and South the sin retain
      Of Yorkist and Lancastrian?

But Rosecrans in the cedarn glade,
   And, deep in denser cypress gloom,
Dark Breckinridge, shall fade away
    Or thinly loom.
The pale throngs who in forest cowed
   Before the spell of battle's pause,
Forefelt the stillness that shall dwell
   On them and on their wars.
      North and South shall join the train
      Of Yorkist and Lancastrian.

But where the sword has plunged so deep,
   And then been turned within the wound
By deadly Hate; where Climes contend
    On vasty ground—
No warning Alps or seas between,
   And small the curb of creed or law,
And blood is quick, and quick the brain;
   Shall North and South their rage deplore,
      And reunited thrive amain
      Like Yorkist and Lancastrian?

Running the Batteries,

As observed from the Anchorage above Vicksburgh.

(APRIL, 1863.)

A MOONLESS night—a friendly one;
　A haze dimmed the shadowy shore
As the first lampless boat slid silent on;
　Hist! and we spake no more;
We but pointed, and stilly, to what we saw.

We felt the dew, and seemed to feel
　The secret like a burden laid.
The first boat melts; and a second keel
　Is blent with the foliaged shade—
Their midnight rounds have the rebel officers made?

Unspied as yet.　A third—a fourth—
　Gun-boat and transport in Indian file
Upon the war-path, smooth from the North;
　But the watch may they hope to beguile?
The manned river-batteries stretch for mile on mile.

A flame leaps out; they are seen;
  Another and another gun roars;
We tell the course of the boats through the screen
  By each further fort that pours,
And we guess how they jump from their beds on those
    shrouded shores.

Converging fires. We speak, though low:
  "That blastful furnace can they thread?"
"Why, Shadrach, Meshach, and Abed-nego
  Came out all right, we read;
The Lord, be sure, he helps his people, Ned."

How we strain our gaze. On bluffs they shun
  A golden growing flame appears—
Confirms to a silvery steadfast one:
  "The town is afire!" crows Hugh: "three cheers!"
Lot stops his mouth: "Nay, lad, better three tears."

A purposed light; it shows our fleet;
  Yet a little late in its searching ray,
So far and strong, that in phantom cheat
  Lank on the deck our shadows lay;
The shining flag-ship stings their guns to furious play.

How dread to mark her near the glare
  And glade of death the beacon throws
Athwart the racing waters there;
  One by one each plainer grows,
Then speeds a blazoned target to our gladdened foes.

The impartial cresset lights as well
  The fixed forts to the boats that run;
And, plunged from the ports, their answers swell
  Back to each fortress dun:
Ponderous words speaks every monster gun.

Fearless they flash through gates of flame,
  The salamanders hard to hit,
Though vivid shows each bulky frame;
  And never the batteries intermit,
Nor the boats huge guns; they fire and flit.

Anon a lull. The beacon dies:
  "Are they out of that strait accurst?"
But other flames now dawning rise,
  Not mellowly brilliant like the first,
But rolled in smoke, whose whitish volumes burst.

A baleful brand, a hurrying torch
   Whereby anew the boats are seen—
A burning transport all alurch!
   Breathless we gaze; yet still we glean
Glimpses of beauty as we eager lean.

The effulgence takes an amber glow
   Which bathes the hill-side villas far;
Affrighted ladies mark the show
   Painting the pale magnolia—
The fair, false, Circe light of cruel War.

The barge drifts doomed, a plague-struck one.
   Shoreward in yawls the sailors fly.
But the gauntlet now is nearly run,
   The spleenful forts by fits reply,
And the burning boat dies down in morning's sky.

All out of range. Adieu, Messieurs!
   Jeers, as it speeds, our parting gun.
So burst we through their barriers
   And menaces every one:
So Porter proves himself a brave man's son.[g]

Stonewall Jackson.

Mortally wounded at Chancellorsville.

(MAY, 1863.)

THE Man who fiercest charged in fight,
  Whose sword and prayer were long—
        Stonewall!
  Even him who stoutly stood for Wrong,
How can we praise? Yet coming days
  Shall not forget him with this song.

Dead is the Man whose Cause is dead,
  Vainly he died and set his seal—
        Stonewall!
  Earnest in error, as we feel;
True to the thing he deemed was due,
  True as John Brown or steel.

Relentlessly he routed us ;
But *we* relent, for he is low—
Stonewall !
Justly his fame we outlaw ; so
We drop a tear on the bold Virginian's bier,
Because no wreath we owe.

Stonewall Jackson.

(Ascribed to a Virginian.)

ONE man we claim of wrought renown
   Which not the North shall care to slur;
A Modern lived who sleeps in death,
   Calm as the marble Ancients are:
      'Tis he whose life, though a vapor's wreath,
      Was charged with the lightning's burning breath—
      Stonewall, stormer of the war.

But who shall hymn the Roman heart?
   A stoic he, but even more :
The iron will and lion thew
   Were strong to inflict as to endure:
      Who like him could stand, or pursue?
      His fate the fatalist followed through;
      In all his great soul found to do
      Stonewall followed his star.

He followed his star on the Romney march
　　Through the sleet to the wintry war;
And·he followed it on when he bowed the grain—
　　The Wind of the Shenandoah;
　　　　At Gaines's Mill in the giants' strain—
　　　　On the fierce forced stride to Manassas-plain,
　　　　Where his sword with thunder was clothed agáin,
　　　　　　Stonewall followed his star.

His star he followed athwart the flood
　　To Potomac's Northern shore,
When midway wading, his host of braves
　　"*My Maryland!*" loud did roar—
　　　　To red Antietam's field of graves,
　　　　Through mountain-passes, woods and waves,
　　　　They followed their pagod with hymns and glaives,
　　　　　　For Stonewall followed a star.

Back it led him to Marye's slope,
　　Where the shock and the fame he bore;
And to green Moss-Neck it guided him—
　　Brief respite from throes of war:
　　　　To the laurel glade by the Wilderness grim,
　　　　Through climaxed victory naught shall dim,
　　　　Even unto death it piloted him—
　　　　　　Stonewall followed his star.

Its lead he followed in gentle ways
  Which never the valiant mar;
A cap we sent him, bestarred, to replace
  The sun-scorched helm of war:
      A fillet he made of the shining lace
      Childhood's laughing brow to grace—
        Not his was a goldsmith's star.

O, much of doubt in after days
  Shall cling, as now, to the war;
Of the right and the wrong they'll still debate,
  Puzzled by Stonewall's star:
      "Fortune went with the North elate,"
      "Ay, but the South had Stonewall's weight,
        And he fell in the South's vain war."

Gettysburg.

The Check.

(July, 1863.)

O PRIDE of the days in prime of the months
  Now trebled in great renown,
When before the ark of our holy cause
    Fell Dagon down—
Dagon foredoomed, who, armed and targed,
Never his impious heart enlarged
Beyond that hour; God walled his power,
And there the last invader charged.

He charged, and in that charge condensed
  His all of hate and all of fire;
He sought to blast us in his scorn,
    And wither us in his ire.
Before him went the shriek of shells—
Aerial screamings, taunts and yells;
Then the three waves in flashed advance

Surged, but were met, and back they set:
Pride was repelled by sterner pride,
    And Right is a strong-hold yet.

Before our lines it seemed a beach
    Which wild September gales have strown
With havoc on wreck, and dashed therewith
      Pale crews unknown—
Men, arms, and steeds. The evening sun
Died on the face of each lifeless one,
And died along the winding marge of fight
      And searching-parties lone.

Sloped on the hill the mounds were green,
    Our centre held that place of graves,
And some still hold it in their swoon,
    And over these a glory waves.
The warrior-monument, crashed in fight,[h]
Shall soar transfigured in loftier light,
      A meaning ampler bear;
Soldier and priest with hymn and prayer
Have laid the stone, and every bone
      Shall rest in honor there.

The House-top.

A Night Piece.

(JULY, 1863.)

No sleep. The sultriness pervades the air
And binds the brain—a dense oppression, such
As tawny tigers feel in matted shades,
Vexing their blood and making apt for ravage.
Beneath the stars the roofy desert spreads
Vacant as Libya. All is hushed near by.
Yet fitfully from far breaks a mixed surf
Of muffled sound, the Atheist roar of riot.
Yonder, where parching Sirius set in drought,
Balefully glares red Arson—there—and there.
The Town is taken by its rats—ship-rats
And rats of the wharves. All civil charms
And priestly spells which late held hearts in awe—
Fear-bound, subjected to a better sway
Than sway of self; these like a dream dissolve,
And man rebounds whole æons back in nature.[i]

Hail to the low dull rumble, dull and dead,
And ponderous drag that shakes the wall.
Wise Draco comes, deep in the midnight˙roll
Of black artillery; he comes, though late;
In code corroborating Calvin's creed
And cynic tyrannies of honest kings;
He comes, nor parlies; and the Town, redeemed,
Gives thanks devout; nor, being thankful, heeds
 The grimy slur on the Republic's faith implied,
Which holds that Man is naturally good,
And—more—is Nature's Roman, never to be scourged.

Look-out Mountain.

The Night Fight.

(NOVEMBER, 1863.)

WHO inhabiteth the Mountain
  That it shines in lurid light,
And is rolled about with thunders,
  And terrors, and a blight,
Like Kaf the peak of Eblis—
  Kaf, the evil height?
Who has gone up with a shouting
  And a trumpet in the night?

There is battle in the Mountain—
  Might assaulteth Might;
'Tis the fastness of the Anarch,
  Torrent-torn, an ancient height;
The crags resound the clangor
  Of the war of Wrong and Right;
And the armies in the valley
  Watch and pray for dawning light.

Joy, joy, the day is breaking,
   And the cloud is rolled from sight;
There is triumph in the Morning
   For the Anarch's plunging flight;
God has glorified the Mountain
   Where a Banner burneth bright,
And the armies in the valley
   They are fortified in right.

Chattanooga.

(November, 1863.)

———————

A KINDLING impulse seized the host
   Inspired by heaven's elastic air;[j]
Their hearts outran their General's plan,
   Though Grant commanded there—
   Grant, who without reserve can dare;
And, "Well, go on and do your will,"
   He said, and measured the mountain then:
So master-riders fling the rein—
   But you must know your men.

On yester-morn in grayish mist,
   Armies like ghosts on hills had fought,
And rolled from the cloud their thunders loud
   The Cumberlands far had caught:
   To-day the sunlit steeps are sought.
Grant stood on cliffs whence all was plain,
   And smoked as one who feels no cares;
But mastered nervousness intense
   Alone such calmness wears.

The summit-cannon plunge their flame
    Sheer down the primal wall,
But up and up each linking troop
    In stretching festoons crawl—
    Nor fire a shot. Such men appall
The foe, though brave. He, from the brink,
    Looks far along the breadth of slope,
And sees two miles of dark dots creep,
    And knows they mean the cope.

He sees them creep. Yet here and there
    Half hid 'mid leafless groves they go ;
As men who ply through traceries high
    Of turreted marbles show—
    So dwindle these to eyes below.
But fronting shot and flanking shell
    Sliver and rive the inwoven ways ;
High tops of oaks and high hearts fall,
    But never the climbing stays.

From right to left, from left to right
    They roll the rallying cheer—
Vie with each other, brother with brother,
    Who shall the first appear—
    What color-bearer with colors clear
In sharp relief, like sky-drawn Grant,

Whose cigar must now be near the stump—
While in solicitude his back
    Heaps slowly to a hump.

Near and more near; till now the flags
    Run like a catching flame;
And one flares highest, to peril nighest—
    He means to make a name:
    Salvos! they give him his fame.
The staff is caught, and next the rush,
    And then the leap where death has led;
Flag answered flag along the crest,
    And swarms of rebels fled.

But some who gained the envied Alp,
    And—eager, ardent, earnest there—
Dropped into Death's wide-open arms,
    Quelled on the wing like eagles struck in air—
    Forever they slumber young and fair,
The smile upon them as they died;
    Their end attained, that end a height:
Life was to these a dream fulfilled,
    And death a starry night.

The Armies of the Wilderness.

(1863–4.)

I.

LIKE snows the camps on Southern hills
  Lay all the winter long,
Our levies there in patience stood—
  They stood in patience strong.
On fronting slopes gleamed other camps
  Where faith as firmly clung:
Ah, froward kin! so brave amiss—
  The zealots of the Wrong.

> *In this strife of brothers*
>   *(God, hear their country call),*
> *However it be, whatever betide,*
>   *Let not the just one fall.*

Through the pointed glass our soldiers saw
  The base-ball bounding sent;

They could have joined them in their sport
  But for the vale's deep rent.
And others turned the reddish soil,
  Like diggers of graves they bent:
The reddish soil and trenching toil
  Begat presentiment.

Did the Fathers feel mistrust?
  Can no final good be wrought?
Over and over, again and again
  Must the fight for the Right be fought?

They lead a Gray-back to the crag:
  "Your earth-works yonder—tell us, man!"
"A prisoner—no deserter, I,
  Nor one of the tell-tale clan."
His rags they mark: "True-blue like you
  Should wear the color—your Country's, man!"
He grinds his teeth: "However that be,
  Yon earth-works have their plan."

Such brave ones, foully snared
  By Belial's wily plea,
Were faithful unto the evil end—
  Feudal fidelity.

"Well, then, your camps—come, tell the names!"
 Freely he leveled his finger then:
"Yonder—see—are our Georgians; on the crest,
 The Carolinians; lower, past the glen,
Virginians—Alabamians—Mississippians—Kentuckians
 (Follow my finger)—Tennesseeans; and the ten
Camps *there*—ask your grave-pits; they'll tell.
 Halloa! I see the picket-hut, the den
Where I last night lay." "Where's Lee?"
"In the hearts and bayonets of all yon men!"

The tribes swarm up to war
As in ages long ago,
Ere the palm of promise leaved
And the lily of Christ did blow.

Their mounted pickets for miles are spied
 Dotting the lowland plain,
The nearer ones in their veteran-rags—
 Loutish they loll in lazy disdain.
But ours in perilous places bide
 With rifles ready and eyes that strain
Deep through the dim suspected wood
 Where the Rapidan rolls amain.

> *The Indian has passed away,*
> *But creeping comes another—*
> *Deadlier far.   Picket,*
> *Take heed—take heed of thy brother!*

From a wood-hung height, an outpost lone,
  Crowned with a woodman's fort,
The sentinel looks on a land of dole,
  Like Paran, all amort.
Black chimneys, gigantic in moor-like wastes,
  The scowl of the clouded sky retort;
The hearth is a houseless stone again—
  Ah! where shall the people be sought?

> *Since the venom such blastment deals,*
> *   The South should have paused, and thrice,*
> *Ere with heat of her hate she hatched*
> *   The egg with the cockatrice.*

A path down the mountain winds to the glade
  Where the dead of the Moonlight Fight lie low;
A hand reaches out of the thin-laid mould
  As begging help which none can bestow.

But the field-mouse small and busy ant
    Heap their hillocks, to hide if they may the woe :
By the bubbling spring lies the rusted canteen,
    And the drum which the drummer-boy dying let go.

> *Dust to dust, and blood for blood—*
>   *Passion and pangs ! Has Time*
> *Gone back ? or is this the Age*
>   *Of the world's great Prime ?*

The wagon mired and cannon dragged
    Have trenched their scar ; the plain
Tramped like the cindery beach of the damned—
    A site for the city of Cain.
And stumps of forests for dreary leagues
    Like a massacre show. The armies have lain
By fires where gums and balms did burn,
    And the seeds of Summer's reign.

> *Where are the birds and boys ?*
>   *Who shall go chestnutting when*
> *October returns ? The nuts—*
>   *O, long ere they grow again.*

E

They snug their huts with the chapel-pews,
   In court-houses stable their steeds—
Kindle their fires with indentures and bonds,
   And old Lord Fairfax's parchment deeds;
And Virginian gentlemen's libraries old—
   Books which only the scholar heeds—
Are flung to his kennel. It is ravage and range,
   And gardens are left to weeds.

> *Turned adrift into war*
> *Man runs wild on the plain,*
> *Like the jennets let loose*
> *On the Pampas—zebras again.*

Like the Pleiads dim, see the tents through the storm—
   Aloft by the hill-side hamlet's graves,
On a head-stone used for a hearth-stone there
   The water is bubbling for punch for our braves.
What if the night be drear, and the blast
   Ghostly shrieks? their rollicking staves
Make frolic the heart; beating time with their swords,
   What care they if Winter raves?

> *Is life but a dream? and so,*
> *In the dream do men laugh aloud?*

So strange seems mirth in a camp,
So like a white tent to a shroud.

II.

The May-weed springs; and comes a Man
  And mounts our Signal Hill;
A quiet Man, and plain in garb—
  Briefly he looks his fill,
Then drops his gray eye on the ground,
  Like a loaded mortar he is still:
Meekness and grimness meet in him—
  The silent General.

Were men but strong and wise,
* Honest as Grant, and calm,*
War would be left to the red and black ants,
* And the happy world disarm.*

That eve a stir was in the camps,
  Forerunning quiet soon to come
Among the streets of beechen huts
  No more to know the drum.
The weed shall choke the lowly door,
  And foxes peer within the gloom,

Till scared perchance by Mosby's prowling men,
  Who ride in the rear of doom.

> *Far West, and farther South,*
>   *Wherever the sword has been,*
> *Deserted camps are met,*
>   *And desert graves are seen.*

The livelong night they ford the flood;
  With guns held high they silent press,
Till shimmers the grass in their bayonets' sheen—
  On Morning's banks their ranks they dress;
Then by the forests lightly wind,
  Whose waving boughs the pennons seem to bless,
Borne by the cavalry scouting on—
  Sounding the Wilderness.

> *Like shoals of fish in spring*
>   *That visit Crusoe's isle,*
> *The host in the lonesome place—*
>   *The hundred thousand file.*

The foe that held his guarded hills
  Must speed to woods afar;

For the scheme that was nursed by the Culpepper hearth
  With the slowly-smoked cigar—
The scheme that smouldered through winter long
  Now bursts into act—into war—
The resolute scheme of a heart as calm
  As the Cyclone's core.

> *The fight for the city is fought*
>   *In Nature's old domain;*
> *Man goes out to the wilds,*
>   *And Orpheus' charm is vain.*

In glades they meet skull after skull
  Where pine-cones lay—the rusted gun,
Green shoes full of bones, the mouldering coat
  And cuddled-up skeleton;
And scores of such. Some start as in dreams,
  And comrades lost bemoan:
By the edge of those wilds Stonewall had charged—
  But the Year and the Man were gone.

> *At the height of their madness*
>   *The night winds pause,*
> *Recollecting themselves;*
>   *But no lull in these wars.*

A gleam!—a volley! And who shall go
  Storming the swarmers in jungles dread?
No cannon-ball answers, no proxies are sent—
  They rush in the shrapnel's stead.
Plume and sash are vanities now—
  Let them deck the pall of the dead;
They go where the shade is, perhaps into Hades,
  Where the brave of all times have led.

> *There's a dust of hurrying feet,*
> *Bitten lips and bated breath,*
> *And drums that challenge to the grave,*
> *And faces fixed, forefeeling death.*

What husky huzzahs in the hazy groves—
  What flying encounters fell;
Pursuer and pursued like ghosts disappear
  In gloomed shade—their end who shall tell?
The crippled, a ragged-barked stick for a crutch,
  Limp to some elfin dell—
Hobble from the sight of dead faces—white
  As pebbles in a well.

> *Few burial rites shall be;*
> *No priest with book and band*

Shall come to the secret place
Of the corpse in the foeman's land.

Watch and fast, march and fight—clutch your gun !
   Day-fights and night-fights ; sore is the stress ;
Look, through the pines what line comes on ?
   Longstreet slants through the hauntedness !
'Tis charge for charge, and shout for yell :
   Such battles on battles oppress—
But Heaven lent strength, the Right strove well,
   And emerged from the Wilderness.

Emerged, for the way was won ;
But the Pillar of Smoke that led
Was brand-like with ghosts that went up
Ashy and red.

None can narrate that strife in the pines,
   A seal is on it—Sabæan lore !
Obscure as the wood, the entangled rhyme
   But hints at the maze of war—
Vivid glimpses or livid through peopled gloom,
   And fires which creep and char—
A riddle of death, of which the slain
   Sole solvers are.

Long they withhold the roll
  Of the shroudless dead. It is right;
Not yet can we bear the flare
  Of the funeral light.

On the Photograph of a Corps Commander.

Ay, man is manly. Here you see
  The warrior-carriage of the head,
And brave dilation of the frame;
  And lighting all, the soul that led
In Spottsylvania's charge to victory,
  Which justifies his fame.

A cheering picture. It is good
  To look upon a Chief like this,
In whom the spirit moulds the form.
  Here favoring Nature, oft remiss,
With eagle mien expressive has endued
  A man to kindle strains that warm.

Trace back his lineage, and his sires,
  Yeoman or noble, you shall find
Enrolled with men of Agincourt,
  Heroes who shared great Harry's mind.

Down to us come the knightly Norman fires,
    And front the Templars bore.

Nothing can lift the heart of man
    Like manhood in a fellow-man.
The thought of heaven's great King afar
    But humbles us—too weak to scan;
But manly greatness men can span,
    And feel the bonds that draw.

*The Swamp Angel.*k

THERE is a coal-black Angel
　With a thick Afric lip,
And he dwells (like the hunted and harried)
　In a swamp where the green frogs dip.
But his face is against a City
　Which is over a bay of the sea,
And he breathes with a breath that is blastment,
　And dooms by a far decree.

By night there is fear in the City,
　Through the darkness a star soareth on ;
There's a scream that screams up to the zenith,
　Then the poise of a meteor lone—
Lighting far the pale fright of the faces,
　And downward the coming is seen ;
Then the rush, and the burst, and the havoc,
　And wails and shrieks between.

It comes like the thief in the gloaming;
　　It comes, and none may foretell
The place of the coming—the glaring;
　　They live in a sleepless spell
That wizens, and withers, and whitens;
　　It ages the young, and the bloom
Of the maiden is ashes of roses—
　　The Swamp Angel broods in his gloom.

Swift is his messengers' going,
　　But slowly he saps their halls,
As if by delay deluding.
　　They move from their crumbling walls
Farther and farther away;
　　But the Angel sends after and after,
By night with the flame of his ray—
　　By night with the voice of his screaming—
Sends after them, stone by stone,
　　And farther walls fall, farther portals,
And weed follows weed through the Town.

Is this the proud City? the scorner
　　Which never would yield the ground?
Which mocked at the coal-black Angel?
　　The cup of despair goes round.

Vainly she calls upon Michael
  (The white man's seraph was he),
For Michael has fled from his tower
  To the Angel over the sea.

Who weeps for the woeful City
  Let him weep for our guilty kind;
Who joys at her wild despairing—
  Christ, the Forgiver, convert his mind.

The Battle for the Bay.

(AUGUST, 1864.)

O MYSTERY of noble hearts,
  To whom mysterious seas have been
In midnight watches, lonely calm and storm,
      A stern, sad discipline,
And rooted out the false and vain,
  And chastened them to aptness for
  Devotion and the deeds of war,
And death which smiles and cheers in spite of pain.

Beyond the bar the land-wind dies,
  The prows becharmed at anchor swim :
A summer night ; the stars withdrawn look down—
      Fair eve of battle grim.
The sentries pace, bonetas glide ;
  Below, the sleeping sailors swing,
  And in their dreams to quarters spring,
Or cheer their flag, or breast a stormy tide.

But drums are beat: *Up anchor all!*
　The triple lines steam slowly on;
Day breaks, and through the sweep of decks each man
　　　Stands coldly by his gun—
As cold as it.　But he shall warm—
　Warm with the solemn metal there,
　And all its ordered fury share,
In attitude a gladiatorial form.

The Admiral—yielding to the love
　Which held his life and ship so dear—
Sailed second in the long fleet's midmost line;
　　　Yet thwarted all their care:
He lashed himself aloft, and shone
　Star of the fight, with influence sent
　Throughout the dusk embattlement;
And so they neared the strait and walls of stone.

No sprightly fife as in the field,
　The decks were hushed like fanes in prayer;
Behind each man a holy angel stood—
　　　He stood, though none was 'ware.
Out spake the forts on either hand,
　Back speak the ships when spoken to,

And set their flags in concert true,
And *On and in!* is Farragut's command.

But what delays? 'mid wounds above
　　Dim buoys give hint of death below—
Sea-ambuscades, where evil art had aped
　　　　Hecla that hides in snow.
The centre-van, entangled, trips ;
　　The starboard leader holds straight on :
　　A cheer for the Tecumseh!—nay,
Before their eyes the turreted ship goes down!

The fire redoubles.　While the fleet
　　Hangs dubious—ere the horror ran—
The Admiral rushes to his rightful place—
　　　　Well met! apt hour and man !—
Closes with peril, takes the lead,
　　His action is a stirring call ;
　　He strikes his great heart through them all,
And is the genius of their daring deed.

The forts are daunted, slack their fire,
　　Confounded by the deadlier aim

And rapid broadsides of the speeding fleet,
 And fierce denouncing flame.
Yet shots from four dark hulls embayed
 Come raking through the loyal crews,
 Whom now each dying mate endues
With his last look, anguished yet undismayed.

A flowering time to guilt is given,
 And traitors have their glorying hour;
O late, but sure, the righteous Paramount comes—
 Palsy is on their power!
So proved it with the rebel keels,
 The strong-holds past: assailed, they run;
 The Selma strikes, and the work is done:
The dropping anchor the achievement seals.

But no, she turns—the Tennessee!
 The solid Ram of iron and oak,
Strong as Evil, and bold as Wrong, though lone—
 A pestilence in her smoke.
The flag-ship is her singled mark,
 The wooden Hartford. Let her come;
 She challenges the planet of Doom,
And naught shall save her—not her iron bark.

Slip anchor, all! and at her, all!
  Bear down with rushing beaks—and now!
First the Monongahela struck—and reeled;
    The Lackawana's prow
Next crashed—crashed, but not crashing; then
  The Admiral rammed, and rasping nigh
  Sloped in a broadside, which glanced by:
The Monitors battered at her adamant den.

The Chickasaw plunged beneath the stern
  And pounded there; a huge wrought orb
From the Manhattan pierced one wall, but dropped;
    Others the seas absorb.
Yet stormed on all sides, narrowed in,
  Hampered and cramped, the bad one fought—
  Spat ribald curses from the port
Whose shutters, jammed, locked up this Man-of-Sin.

No pause or stay. They made a din
  Like hammers round a boiler forged;
Now straining strength tangled itself with strength,
  Till Hate her will disgorged.
The white flag showed, the fight was won—
  Mad shouts went up that shook the Bay;

But pale on the scarred fleet's decks there lay
A silent man for every silenced gun.

And quiet far below the wave,
  Where never cheers shall move their sleep,
Some who did boldly, nobly earn them, lie—
    Charmed children of the deep.
But decks that now are in the seed,
  And cannon yet within the mine,
  Shall thrill the deeper, gun and pine,
Because of the Tecumseh's glorious deed.

Sheridan at Cedar Creek.

(OCTOBER, 1864.)

SHOE the steed with silver
  That bore him to the fray,
When he heard the guns at dawning—
    Miles away;
When he heard them calling, calling—
    Mount! nor stay:
      Quick, or all is lost;
      They've surprised and stormed the post,
      They push your routed host—
Gallop! retrieve the day.

House the horse in ermine—
  For the foam-flake blew
White through the red October;
  He thundered into view;
They cheered him in the looming,
  Horseman and horse they knew.

The turn of the tide began,
    The rally of bugles ran,
    He swung his hat in the van;
The electric hoof-spark flew.

Wreathe the steed and lead him—
    For the charge he led
Touched and turned the cypress
    Into amaranths for the head
Of Philip, king of riders,
    Who raised them from the dead.
        The camp (at dawning lost),
        By eve, recovered—forced,
        Rang with laughter of the host
At belated Early fled.

Shroud the horse in sable—
    For the mounds they heap!
There is firing in the Valley,
    And yet no strife they keep;
It is the parting volley,
    It is the pathos deep.
        There is glory for the brave
        Who lead, and nobly save,
        But no knowledge in the grave
Where the nameless followers sleep.

In the Prison Pen.

(1864.)

LISTLESS he eyes the palisades
　　And sentries in the glare;
'Tis barren as a pelican-beach—
　　But his world is ended there.

Nothing to do; and vacant hands
　　Bring on the idiot-pain;
He tries to think—to recollect,
　　But the blur is on his brain.

Around him swarm the plaining ghosts
　　Like those on Virgil's shore—
A wilderness of faces dim,
　　And pale ones gashed and hoar.

A smiting sun.　No shed, no tree;
　　He totters to his lair—
A den that sick hands dug in earth
　　Ere famine wasted there,

Or, dropping in his place, he swoons,
    Walled in by throngs that press,
Till forth from the throngs they bear him dead—
    Dead in his meagreness.

The College Colonel.

HE rides at their head;
  A crutch by his saddle just slants in view,
One slung arm is in splints, you see,
  Yet he guides his strong steed—how coldly too.

He brings his regiment home—
  Not as they filed two years before,
But a remnant half-tattered, and battered, and worn,
Like castaway sailors, who—stunned
    By the surf's loud roar,
  Their mates dragged back and seen no more—
Again and again breast the surge,
  And at last crawl, spent, to shore.

A still rigidity and pale—
  An Indian aloofness lones his brow;
He has lived a thousand years
Compressed in battle's pains and prayers,
  Marches and watches slow.

There are welcoming shouts, and flags ;
   Old men off hat to the Boy,
Wreaths from gay balconies fall at his feet,
   But to *him*—there comes alloy.

It is not that a leg is lost,
   It is not that an arm is maimed,
It is not that the fever has racked—
   Self he has long disclaimed.

But all through the Seven Days' Fight,
   And deep in the Wilderness grim,
And in the field-hospital tent,
   And Petersburg crater, and dim
Lean brooding in Libby, there came—
   Ah heaven !—what *truth* to him.

F

The Eagle of the Blue.[1]

Aloft he guards the starry folds
  Who is the brother of the star;
The bird whose joy is in the wind
  Exulteth in the war.

No painted plume—a sober hue,
  His beauty is his power;
That eager calm of gaze intent
  Foresees the Sibyl's hour.

Austere, he crowns the swaying perch,
  Flapped by the angry flag;
The hurricane from the battery sings,
  But his claw has known the crag.

Amid the scream of shells, his scream
  Runs shrilling; and the glare
Of eyes that brave the blinding sun
  The vollied flame can bear.

The pride of quenchless strength is his—
  Strength which, though chained, avails;
The very rebel looks and thrills—
  The anchored Emblem hails.

Though scarred in many a furious fray,
  No deadly hurt he knew;
Well may we think his years are charmed—
  The Eagle of the Blue.

A Dirge for McPherson,[m]

Killed in front of Atlanta.

(July, 1864.)

———————————

ARMS reversed and banners craped—
    Muffled drums ;
Snowy horses sable-draped—
    McPherson comes.

    But, tell us, shall we know him more,
    Lost-Mountain and lone Kenesaw ?

Brave the sword upon the pall—
    A gleam in gloom ;
So a bright name lighteth all
    McPherson's doom.

Bear him through the chapel-door—
    Let priest in stole
Pace before the warrior
    Who led. Bell—toll !

Lay him down within the nave,
  The Lesson read—
Man is noble, man is brave,
  But man's—a weed.

Take him up again and wend
  Graveward, nor weep:
There's a trumpet that shall rend
  This Soldier's sleep.

Pass the ropes the coffin round,
  And let descend;
Prayer and volley—let it sound
  McPherson's end.

  True fame is his, for life is o'er—
  Sarpedon of the mighty war.

At the Cannon's Mouth.

Destruction of the Ram Albemarle by the Torpedo-launch.

(OCTOBER, 1864.)

PALELY intent, he urged his keel
    Full on the guns, and touched the spring;
Himself involved in the bolt he drove
Timed with the armed hull's shot that stove
His shallop—die or do!
Into the flood his life he threw,
    Yet lives—unscathed—a breathing thing
To marvel at.

        He has his fame;
But that mad dash at death, how name?

Had Earth no charm to stay the Boy
    From the martyr-passion? Could he dare
Disdain the Paradise of opening joy
    Which beckons the fresh heart every where?
Life has more lures than any girl
    For youth and strength; puts forth a share

Of beauty, hinting of yet rarer store;
And ever with unfathomable eyes,
    Which bafflingly entice,
Still strangely does Adonis draw.
And life once over, who shall tell the rest?
Life is, of all we know, God's best.
What imps these eagles then, that they
Fling disrespect on life by that proud way
In which they soar above our lower clay.

Pretense of wonderment and doubt unblest:
    In Cushing's eager deed was shown
    A spirit which brave poets own—
That scorn of life which earns life's crown;
    Earns, but not always wins; but *he*—
    The star ascended in his nativity.

The March to the Sea.

(DECEMBER, 1864.)

NOT Kenesaw high-arching,
  Nor Allatoona's glen—
Though there the graves lie parching—
  Stayed Sherman's miles of men;
From charred Atlanta marching
  They launched the sword again.
      The columns streamed like rivers
        Which in their course agree,
      And they streamed until their flashing
        Met the flashing of the sea:
          It was glorious glad marching,
          That marching to the sea.

They brushed the foe before them
  (Shall gnats impede the bull?);
Their own good bridges bore them
  Over swamps or torrents full,

And the grand pines waving o'er them
  Bowed to axes keen and cool.
    The columns grooved their channels,
      Enforced their own decree,
    And their power met nothing larger
      Until it met the sea:
        It was glorious glad marching,
        A marching glad and free.

Kilpatrick's snare of riders
  In zigzags mazed the land,
Perplexed the pale Southsiders
  With feints on every hand;
Vague menace awed the hiders
  In forts beyond command.
    To Sherman's shifting problem
      No foeman knew the key;
    But onward went the marching
      Unpausing to the sea:
        It was glorious glad marching,
        The swinging step was free.

The flankers ranged like pigeons
  In clouds through field or wood;

The flocks of all those regions,
  The herds and horses good,
Poured in and swelled the legions,
  For they caught the marching mood.
        A volley ahead! They hear it;
          And they hear the repartee:
        Fighting was but frolic
          In that marching to the sea:
              It was glorious glad marching,
              A marching bold and free.

All nature felt their coming,
  The birds like couriers flew,
And the banners brightly blooming
  The slaves by thousands drew,
And they marched beside the drumming,
  And they joined the armies blue.
        The cocks crowed from the cannon
          (Pets named from Grant and Lee),
        Plumed fighters and campaigners
          In that marching to the sea:
              It was glorious glad marching,
              For every man was free.

The foragers through calm lands
  Swept in tempest gay,
And they breathed the air of balm-lands
  Where rolled savannas lay,
And they helped themselves from farm-lands—
  As who should say them nay?
     The regiments uproarious
      Laughed in Plenty's glee;
     And they marched till their broad laughter
      Met the laughter of the sea:
        It was glorious glad marching,
        That marching to the sea.

The grain of endless acres
  Was threshed (as in the East)
By the trampling of the Takers,
  Strong march of man and beast;
The flails of those earth-shakers
  Left a famine where they ceased.
     The arsenals were yielded;
      The sword (that was to be),
     Arrested in the forging,
      Rued that marching to the sea:
        It was glorious glad marching,
        But ah, the stern decree!

For behind they left a wailing,
   A terror and a ban,
And blazing cinders sailing,
   And houseless households wan,
Wide zones of counties paling,
   And towns where maniacs ran.
        Was it Treason's retribution—
        Necessity the plea?
       They will long remember Sherman
        And his streaming columns free—
         They will long remember Sherman
         Marching to the sea.

The Frenzy in the Wake.[n]

Sherman's advance through the Carolinas.

(FEBRUARY, 1865.)

So strong to suffer, shall we be
  Weak to contend, and break
The sinews of the Oppressor's knee
  That grinds upon the neck?
     O, the garments rolled in blood
      Scorch in cities wrapped in flame,
     And the African—the imp!
     He gibbers, imputing shame.

Shall Time, avenging every woe,
  To us that joy allot
Which Israel thrilled when Sisera's brow
  Showed gaunt and showed the clot?
     Curse on their foreheads, cheeks, and eyes—
      The Northern faces—true
     To the flag we hate, the flag whose stars
     Like planets strike us through.

From frozen Maine they come,
　Far Minnesota too ;
They come to a sun whose rays disown—
　May it wither them as the dew !
　　The ghosts of our slain appeal :
　　"Vain shall our victories be?"
　　But back from its ebb the flood recoils—
　　Back in a whelming sea.

With burning woods our skies are brass,
　The pillars of dust are seen ;
The live-long day their cavalry pass—
　No crossing the road between.
　　We were sore deceived—an awful host !
　　They move like a roaring wind.
　　Have we gamed and lost? but even despair
　　Shall never our hate rescind.

The Fall of Richmond.

The tidings received in the Northern Metropolis.

(APRIL, 1865.)

WHAT mean these peals from every tower,
  And crowds like seas that sway?
The cannon reply; they speak the heart
  Of the People impassioned, and say—
A city in flags for a city in flames,
  Richmond goes Babylon's way—
    Sing and pray.

O weary years and woeful wars,
  And armies in the grave;
But hearts unquelled at last deter
The helmed dilated Lucifer—
  Honor to Grant the brave,
Whose three stars now like Orion's rise
  When wreck is on the wave—
    Bless his glaive.

Well that the faith we firmly kept,
　　And never our aim forswore
For the Terrors that trooped from each recess
When fainting we fought in the Wilderness,
　　And Hell made loud hurrah ;
But God is in Heaven, and Grant in the Town,
　　And Right through might is Law—
　　　　God's way adore.

The Surrender at Appomattox.

(APRIL, 1865.)

As billows upon billows roll,
  On victory victory breaks;
Ere yet seven days from Richmond's fall
  And crowning triumph wakes
The loud joy-gun, whose thunders run
  By sea-shore, streams, and lakes.
    The hope and great event agree
      In the sword that Grant received from Lee.

The warring eagles fold the wing,
  But not in Cæsar's sway;
Not Rome o'ercome by Roman arms we sing,
  As on Pharsalia's day,
But Treason thrown, though a giant grown,
  And Freedom's larger play.
    All human tribes glad token see
      In the close of the wars of Grant and Lee.

A Canticle:

Significant of the national exaltation of enthusiasm at the close of the War.

O THE precipice Titanic
  Of the congregated Fall,
And the angle oceanic
  Where the deepening thunders call—
    And the Gorge so grim,
    And the firmamental rim!
Multitudinously thronging
  The waters all converge,
Then they sweep adown in sloping
  Solidity of surge.

    The Nation, in her impulse
      Mysterious as the Tide,
    In emotion like an ocean
      Moves in power, not in pride;
    And is deep in her devotion
      As Humanity is wide.

Thou Lord of hosts victorious,
  The confluence Thou hast twined ;
By a wondrous way and glorious
  A passage Thou dost find—
  A passage Thou dost find :
Hosanna to the Lord of hosts,
  The hosts of human kind.

Stable in its baselessness
  When calm is in the air,
The Iris half in tracelessness
  Hovers faintly fair.
Fitfully assailing it
  A wind from heaven blows,
Shivering and paling it
  To blankness of the snows ;
While, incessant in renewal,
  The Arch rekindled grows,
Till again the gem and jewel
  Whirl in blinding overthrows—
Till, prevailing and transcending,
  Lo, the Glory perfect there,
And the contest finds an ending,
  For repose is in the air.

But the foamy Deep unsounded,
　　And the dim and dizzy ledge,
And the booming roar rebounded,
　　And the gull that skims the edge!
　　　The Giant of the Pool
　　　Heaves his forehead white as wool—
Toward the Iris ever climbing
　　From the Cataracts that call—
Irremovable vast arras
　　Draping all the Wall.

　　　The Generations pouring
　　　　From times of endless date,
　　In their going, in their flowing
　　　Ever form the steadfast State;
　　And Humanity is growing
　　　Toward the fullness of her fate.

　　　　Thou Lord of hosts victorious,
　　　　　Fulfill the end designed;
　　　By a wondrous way and glorious
　　　　A passage Thou dost find—
　　　　A passage Thou dost find:
　　　Hosanna to the Lord of hosts,
　　　　The hosts of human kind.

The Martyr.

Indicative of the passion of the people on the 15th of
April, 1865.

GOOD Friday was the day
  Of the prodigy and crime,
When they killed him in his pity,
  When they killed him in his prime
Of clemency and calm—
    When with yearning he was filled
    To redeem the evil-willed,
And, though conqueror, be kind;
  But they killed him in his kindness,
  In their madness and their blindness,
And they killed him from behind.

      There is sobbing of the strong,
      And a pall upon the land;
      But the People in their weeping
        Bare the iron hand:
      Beware the People weeping
      When they bare the iron hand.

He lieth in his blood—
   The father in his face;
They have killed him, the Forgiver—
   The Avenger takes his place,°
The Avenger wisely stern,
     Who in righteousness shall do
     What the heavens call him to,
And the parricides remand;
    For they killed him in his kindness,
    In their madness and their blindness,
And his blood is on their hand.

       There is sobbing of the strong,
        And a pall upon the land;
       But the People in their weeping
          Bare the iron hand:
       Beware the People weeping
        When they bare the iron hand.

"*The Coming Storm:*"

*A Picture by S. R. Gifford, and owned by E. B.   Included
in the N. A. Exhibition, April,* 1865.

———————

ALL feeling hearts must feel for him
    Who felt this picture. Presage dim—
Dim inklings from the shadowy sphere
    Fixed him and fascinated here.

A demon-cloud like the mountain one
    Burst on a spirit as mild
As this urned lake, the home of shades.
    But Shakspeare's pensive child

Never the lines had lightly scanned,
    Steeped in fable, steeped in fate;
The Hamlet in his heart was 'ware,
    Such hearts can antedate.

No utter surprise can come to him
    Who reaches Shakspeare's core;
That which we seek and shun is there—
    Man's final lore.

Rebel Color-bearers at Shiloh :[p]

*A plea against the vindictive cry raised by civilians shortly
after the surrender at Appomattox.*

THE color-bearers facing death
White in the whirling sulphurous wreath,
  Stand boldly out before the line;
Right and left their glances go,
Proud of each other, glorying in their show;
Their battle-flags about them blow,
  And fold them as in flame divine:
Such living robes are only seen
Round martyrs burning on the green—
And martyrs for the Wrong have been.

Perish their Cause! but mark the men—
Mark the planted statues, then
Draw trigger on them if you can.

The leader of a patriot-band
Even so could view rebels who so could stand;

And this when peril pressed him sore,
Left aidless in the shivered front of war—
  Skulkers behind, defiant foes before,
And fighting with a broken brand.
The challenge in that courage rare—
Courage defenseless, proudly bare—
Never could tempt him ; he could dare
Strike up the leveled rifle there.

Sunday at Shiloh, and the day
When Stonewall charged—McClellan's crimson May,
And Chickamauga's wave of death,
And of the Wilderness the cypress wreath—
  All these have passed away.
The life in the veins of Treason lags,
Her daring color-bearers drop their flags,
  And yield. *Now* shall we fire ?
    Can poor spite be ?
Shall nobleness in victory less aspire
Than in reverse ? Spare Spleen her ire,
  And think how Grant met Lee.

G

The Muster :[q]

Suggested by the Two Days' Review at Washington.

(MAY, 1865.)

———————

THE Abrahamic river—
  Patriarch of floods,
Calls the roll of all his streams
  And watery multitudes :
        Torrent cries to torrent,
          The rapids hail the fall ;
        With shouts the inland freshets
          Gather to the call.

    The quotas of the Nation,
      Like the water-shed of waves,
    Muster into union—
      Eastern warriors, Western braves.

Martial strains are mingling,
  Though distant far the bands,
And the wheeling of the squadrons
  Is like surf upon the sands.

The bladed guns are gleaming—
  Drift in lengthened trim,
Files on files for hazy miles—
  Nebulously dim.

O Milky Way of armies—
  Star rising after star,
New banners of the Commonwealths,
  And eagles of the War.

The Abrahamic river
  To sea-wide fullness fed,
Pouring from the thaw-lands
  By the God of floods is led:
      His deep enforcing current
        The streams of ocean own,
      And Europe's marge is evened
        By rills from Kansas lone.

Aurora-Borealis.

Commemorative of the Dissolution of Armies at the Peace.

(MAY, 1865.)

WHAT power disbands the Northern Lights
  After their steely play?
The lonely watcher feels an awe
  Of Nature's sway,
    As when appearing,
    He marked their flashed uprearing
In the cold gloom—
  Retreatings and advancings,
(Like dallyings of doom),
  Transitions and enhancings,
    And bloody ray.

The phantom-host has faded quite,
  Splendor and Terror gone—
Portent or promise—and gives way
  To pale, meek Dawn;

The coming, going,
Alike in wonder showing—
Alike the God,
Decreeing and commanding
The million blades that glowed,
The muster and disbanding—
Midnight and Morn.

The Released Rebel Prisoner.

(June, 1865.)

Armies he's seen—the herds of war,
    But never such swarms of men
As now in the Nineveh of the North—
    How mad the Rebellion then!

And yet but dimly he divines
    The depth of that deceit,
And superstition of vast pride
    Humbled to such defeat.

Seductive shone the Chiefs in arms—
    His steel the nearest magnet drew;
Wreathed with its kind, the Gulf-weed drives—
    'Tis Nature's wrong they rue.

His face is hidden in his beard,
    But his heart peers out at eye—

And such a heart! like a mountain-pool
    Where no man passes by.

He thinks of Hill—a brave soul gone;
    And Ashby dead in pale disdain;
And Stuart with the Rupert-plume,
    Whose blue eye never shall laugh again.

He hears the drum; he sees our boys
    From his wasted fields return;
Ladies feast them on strawberries,
    And even to kiss them yearn.

He marks them bronzed, in soldier-trim,
    The rifle proudly borne;
They bear it for an heir-loom home,
    And he—disarmed—jail-worn.

Home, home—his heart is full of it;
    But home he never shall see,
Even should he stand upon the spot:
    'Tis gone!—where his brothers be.

The cypress-moss from tree to tree
    Hangs in his Southern land ;
As wierd, from thought to thought of his
    Run memories hand in hand.

And so he lingers—lingers on
    In the City of the Foe—
His cousins and his countrymen
    Who see him listless go.

A Grave near Petersburg, Virginia.

HEAD-BOARD and foot-board duly placed—
   Grassed is the mound between;
Daniel Drouth is the slumberer's name—
   Long may his grave be green!

Quick was his way—a flash and a blow,
   Full of his fire was he—
A fire of hell—'tis burnt out now—
   Green may his grave long be!

May his grave be green, though he
   Was a rebel of iron mould;
Many a true heart—true to the Cause,
   Through the blaze of his wrath lies cold.

May his grave be green—still green
   While happy years shall run;
May none come nigh to disinter
   The—*Buried Gun.*

"*Formerly a Slave.*"

An idealized Portrait, by E. Vedder, in the Spring Exhibition of the National Academy, 1865.

———————

THE sufferance of her race is shown,
    And retrospect of life,
Which now too late deliverance dawns upon;
    Yet is she not at strife.

Her children's children they shall know
    The good withheld from her;
And so her reverie takes prophetic cheer—
    In spirit she sees the stir

Far down the depth of thousand years,
    And marks the revel shine;
Her dusky face is lit with sober light,
    Sibylline, yet benign.

The Apparition.

(A Retrospect.)

CONVULSIONS came; and, where the field
    Long slept in pastoral green,
A goblin-mountain was upheaved
(Sure the scared sense was all deceived),
    Marl-glen and slag-ravine.

The unreserve of Ill was there,
    The clinkers in her last retreat;
But, ere the eye could take it in,
Or mind could comprehension win,
    It sunk!—and at our feet.

So, then, Solidity's a crust—
    The core of fire below;
All may go well for many a year,
But who can think without a fear
    Of horrors that happen so?

Magnanimity Baffled.

"Sharp words we had before the fight;
     But—now the fight is done—
Look, here's my hand," said the Victor bold,
     "Take it—an honest one!
What, holding back? I mean you well;
   Though worsted, you strove stoutly, man;
The odds were great; I honor you;
          Man honors man.

"Still silent, friend? can grudges be?
     Yet am I held a foe?—
Turned to the wall, on his cot he lies—
     Never I'll leave him so!
Brave one! I here implore your hand;
   Dumb still? all fellowship fled?
Nay, then, I'll have this stubborn hand!"
     He snatched it—it was dead.

On the Slain Collegians.[t]

YOUTH is the time when hearts are large,
   And stirring wars
Appeal to the spirit which appeals in turn
   To the blade it draws.
If woman incite, and duty show
   (Though made the mask of Cain),
Or whether it be Truth's sacred cause,
   Who can aloof remain
That shares youth's ardor, uncooled by the snow
   Of wisdom or sordid gain?

The liberal arts and nurture sweet
Which give his gentleness to man—
   Train him to honor, lend him grace
Through bright examples meet—
That culture which makes never wan
With underminings deep, but holds
   The surface still, its fitting place,
   And so gives sunniness to the face

And bravery to the heart ; what troops
  Of generous boys in happiness thus bred—
  Saturnians through life's Tempe led,
Went from the North and came from the South,
With golden mottoes in the mouth,
  To lie down midway on a bloody bed.

Woe for the homes of the North,
And woe for the seats of the South :
All who felt life's spring in prime,
And were swept by the wind of their place and time—
  All lavish hearts, on whichever side,
Of birth urbane or courage high,
Armed them for the stirring wars—
Armed them—some to die.
      Apollo-like in pride,
Each would slay his Python—caught
The maxims in his temple taught—
  Aflame with sympathies whose blaze
Perforce enwrapped him—social laws,
  Friendship and kin, and by-gone days—
Vows, kisses—every heart unmoors,
And launches into the seas of wars.
What could they else—North or South ?
Each went forth with blessings given

By priests and mothers in the name of Heaven;
    And honor in both was chief.
Warred one for Right, and one for Wrong?
So be it; but they both were young—
Each grape to his cluster clung,
All their elegies are sung.

The anguish of maternal hearts
  Must search for balm divine;
But well the striplings bore their fated parts
  (The heavens all parts assign)—
Never felt life's care or cloy.
Each bloomed and died an unabated Boy;
Nor dreamed what death was—thought it mere
Sliding into some vernal sphere.
They knew the joy, but leaped the grief,
Like plants that flower ere comes the leaf—
Which storms lay low in kindly doom,
And kill them in their flush of bloom.

America.

I.

WHERE the wings of a sunny Dome expand
I saw a Banner in gladsome air—
Starry, like Berenice's Hair—
Afloat in broadened bravery there;
With undulating long-drawn flow,
As rolled Brazilian billows go
Voluminously o'er the Line.
The Land reposed in peace below;
    The children in their glee
Were folded to the exulting heart
    Of young Maternity.

II.

Later, and it streamed in fight
    When tempest mingled with the fray,
And over the spear-point of the shaft
    I saw the ambiguous lightning play.
Valor with Valor strove, and died:
Fierce was Despair, and cruel was Pride;

And the lorn Mother speechless stood,
Pale at the fury of her brood.

III.

Yet later, and the silk did wind
    Her fair cold form;
Little availed the shining shroud,
    Though ruddy in hue, to cheer or warm.
A watcher looked upon her low, and said—
She sleeps, but sleeps, she is not dead.
    But in that sleep contortion showed
The terror of the vision there—
    A silent vision unavowed,
Revealing earth's foundation bare,
    And Gorgon in her hidden place.
It was a thing of fear to see
    So foul a dream upon so fair a face,
And the dreamer lying in that starry shroud.

IV.

But from the trance she sudden broke—
    The trance, or death into promoted life;
At her feet a shivered yoke,
    And in her aspect turned to heaven
    No trace of passion or of strife—

A clear calm look. It spake of pain,
But such as purifies from stain—
Sharp pangs that never come again—
 And triumph repressed by knowledge meet,
Power dedicate, and hope grown wise,
 And youth matured for age's seat—
Law on her brow and empire in her eyes.
 So she, with graver air and lifted flag;
While the shadow, chased by light,
Fled along the far-drawn height,
 And left her on the crag.

VERSES

INSCRIPTIVE AND MEMORIAL.

On the Home Guards

who perished in the Defense of Lexington, Missouri.

THE men who here in harness died
    Fell not in vain, though in defeat.
They by their end well fortified
    The Cause, and built retreat
(With memory of their valor tried)
For emulous hearts in many an after fray—
Hearts sore beset, which died at bay.

Inscription

for Graves at Pea Ridge, Arkansas.

Let none misgive we died amiss
  When here we strove in furious fight:
Furious it was; nathless was this
  Better than tranquil plight,
And tame surrender of the Cause
Hallowed by hearts and by the laws.
  We here who warred for Man and Right,
The choice of warring never laid with us.
  There we were ruled by the traitor's choice.
  Nor long we stood to trim and poise,
But marched, and fell—victorious!

The Fortitude of the North
under the Disaster of the Second Manassas.

THEY take no shame for dark defeat
 While prizing yet each victory won,
Who fight for the Right through all retreat,
 Nor pause until their work is done.
The Cape-of-Storms is proof to every throe;
 Vainly against that foreland beat
Wild winds aloft and wilder waves below :
 The black cliffs gleam through rents in sleet
When the livid Antarctic storm-clouds glow.

On the Men of Maine

killed in the Victory of Baton Rouge, Louisiana.

AFAR they fell. It was the zone
  Of fig and orange, cane and lime
(A land how all unlike their own,
With the cold pine-grove overgrown),
  But still their Country's clime.
And there in youth they died for her—
    The Volunteers,
For her went up their dying prayers :
  So vast the Nation, yet so strong the tie.
What doubt shall come, then, to deter
  The Republic's earnest faith and courage high.

An Epitaph.

WHEN Sunday tidings from the front
 Made pale the priest and people,
And heavily the blessing went,
 And bells were dumb in the steeple;
The Soldier's widow (summering sweetly here,
 In shade by waving beeches lent)
Felt deep at heart her faith content,
And priest and people borrowed of her cheer.

H

Inscription

for Maryè's Heights, Fredericksburg.

To them who crossed the flood
And climbed the hill, with eyes
   Upon the heavenly flag intent,
   And through the deathful tumult went
Even unto death : to them this Stone—
Erect, where they were overthrown—
   Of more than victory the monument.

The Mound by the Lake.

THE grass shall never forget this grave.
When homeward footing it in the sun
    After the weary ride by rail,
The stripling soldiers passed her door,
    Wounded perchance, or wan and pale,
She left her household work undone—
Duly the wayside table spread,
    With evergreens shaded, to regale
Each travel-spent and grateful one.
So warm her heart—childless—unwed,
Who like a mother comforted.

On the Slain at Chickamauga.

HAPPY are they and charmed in life
  Who through long wars arrive unscarred
At peace. To such the wreath be given,
If they unfalteringly have striven—
  In honor, as in limb, unmarred.
Let cheerful praise be rife,
  And let them live their years at ease,
Musing on brothers who victorious died—
  Loved mates whose memory shall ever please.

And yet mischance is honorable too—
  Seeming defeat in conflict justified
Whose end to closing eyes is hid from view.
The will, that never can relent—
The aim, survivor of the bafflement,
    Make this memorial due.

An uninscribed Monument

on one of the Battle-fields of the Wilderness.

SILENCE and Solitude may hint
   (Whose home is in yon piny wood)
What I, though tableted, could never tell—
The din which here befell,
   And striving of the multitude.
The iron cones and spheres of death
   Set round me in their rust,
      These, too, if just,
Shall speak with more than animated breath.
   Thou who beholdest, if thy thought,
Not narrowed down to personal cheer,
Take in the import of the quiet here—
   The after-quiet—the calm full fraught ;
Thou too wilt silent stand—
Silent as I, and lonesome as the land.

On Sherman's Men

who fell in the Assault of Kenesaw Mountain, Georgia.

THEY said that Fame her clarion dropped
    Because great deeds were done no more—
That even Duty knew no shining ends,
And Glory—'twas a fallen star!
    But battle can heroes and bards restore.
        Nay, look at Kenesaw:
Perils the mailed ones never knew
Are lightly braved by the ragged coats of blue,
And gentler hearts are bared to deadlier war.

On the Grave

of a young Cavalry Officer killed in the Valley of Virginia.

BEAUTY and youth, with manners sweet, and friends—
  Gold, yet a mind not unenriched had he
Whom here low violets veil from eyes.
  But all these gifts transcended be :
His happier fortune in this mound you see.

A Requiem

for Soldiers lost in Ocean Transports.

WHEN, after storms that woodlands rue,
　To valleys comes atoning dawn,
The robins blithe their orchard-sports renew;
　And meadow-larks, no more withdrawn,
Caroling fly in the languid blue;
The while, from many a hid recess,
Alert to partake the blessedness,
The pouring mites their airy dance pursue.
　So, after ocean's ghastly gales,
When laughing light of hoyden morning breaks,
　　Every finny hider wakes—
　From vaults profound swims up with glittering scales;
　Through the delightsome sea he sails,
With shoals of shining tiny things
Frolic on every wave that flings
　Against the prow its showery spray;
All creatures joying in the morn,
Save them forever from joyance torn,
　Whose bark was lost where now the dolphins play;

Save them that by the fabled shore,
  Down the pale stream are washed away,
Far to the reef of bones are borne ;
  And never revisits them the light,
Nor sight of long-sought land and pilot more ;
  Nor heed they now the lone bird's flight
Round the lone spar where mid-sea surges pour.

H 2

On a natural Monument

in a field of Georgia.[u]

No trophy this—a Stone unhewn,
  And stands where here the field immures
The nameless brave whose palms are won.
Outcast they sleep; yet fame is nigh—
  Pure fame of deeds, not doers;
Nor deeds of men who bleeding die
  In cheer of hymns that round them float:
In happy dreams such close the eye.
But withering famine slowly wore,
  And slowly fell disease did gloat.
Even Nature's self did aid deny;
They choked in horror the pensive sigh.
  Yea, off from home sad Memory bore
(Though anguished Yearning heaved that way),
Lest wreck of reason might befall.
  As men in gales shun the lee shore,
Though there the homestead be, and call,
And thitherward winds and waters sway—
As such lorn mariners, so fared they.

But naught shall now their peace molest.
　Their fame is this : they did endure—
Endure, when fortitude was vain
To kindle any approving strain
Which they might hear.　To these who rest,
　This healing sleep alone was sure.

Commemorative of a Naval Victory.

SAILORS there are of gentlest breed,
   Yet 'strong, like every goodly thing;
The discipline of arms refines,
   And the wave gives tempering.
   The damasked blade its beam can fling;
It lends the last grave grace:
The hawk, the hound, and sworded nobleman
   In Titian's picture for a king,
Are of hunter or warrior race.

In social halls a favored guest
   In years that follow victory won,
How sweet to feel your festal fame
   In woman's glance instinctive thrown:
   Repose is yours—your deed is known,
It musks the amber wine;
It lives, and sheds a light from storied days
   Rich as October sunsets brown,
Which make the barren place to shine.

But seldom the laurel wreath is seen
    Unmixed with pensive pansies dark;
There's a light and a shadow on every man
    Who at last attains his lifted mark—
    Nursing through night the ethereal spark.
Elate he never can be;
He feels that spirits which glad had hailed his worth,
    Sleep in oblivion.—The shark
Glides white through the phosphorus sea.

Presentation to the Authorities,

by Privates, of Colors captured in Battles ending in the Surrender of Lee.

THESE flags of armies overthrown—
Flags fallen beneath the sovereign one
In end foredoomed which closes war;
We here, the captors, lay before
  The altar which of right claims all—
Our Country. And as freely we,
  Revering ever her sacred call,
Could lay our lives down—though life be
Thrice loved and precious to the sense
Of such as reap the recompense
  Of life imperiled for just cause—
Imperiled, and yet preserved;
While comrades, whom Duty as strongly nerved,
Whose wives were all as dear, lie low.
But these flags given, glad we go
  To waiting homes with vindicated laws.

The Returned Volunteer to his Rifle.

OVER this hearth—my father's seat—
  Repose, to patriot-memory dear,
Thou tried companion, whom at last I greet
  By steepy banks of Hudson here.
How oft I told thee of this scene—
The Highlands blue—the river's narrowing sheen.
Little at Gettysburg we thought
To find such haven ; but God kept it green.
Long rest! with belt, and bayonet, and canteen.

THE SCOUT TOWARD ALDIE.

The Scout toward Aldie.

THE cavalry-camp lies on the slope
    Of what was late a vernal hill,
But now like a pavement bare—
An outpost in the perilous wilds
    Which ever are lone and still;
        But Mosby's men are there—
        Of Mosby best beware.

Great trees the troopers felled, and leaned
    In antlered walls about their tents;
Strict watch they kept; 'twas *Hark!* and *Mark!*
Unarmed none cared to stir abroad
    For berries beyond their forest-fence:
        As glides in seas the shark,
        Rides Mosby through green dark.

All spake of him, but few had seen
    Except the maimed ones or the low;
Yet rumor made him every thing—
A farmer—woodman—refugee—
    The man who crossed the field but now;
        A spell about his life did cling—
        Who to the ground shall Mosby bring?

The morning-bugles lonely play,
    Lonely the evening-bugle calls—
Unanswered voices in the wild;
The settled hush of birds in nest
    Becharms, and all the wood enthralls:
        Memory's self is so beguiled
        That Mosby seems a satyr's child.

They lived as in the Eerie Land—
    The fire-flies showed with fairy gleam;
And yet from pine-tops one might ken
The Capitol Dome—hazy—sublime—
    A vision breaking on a dream:
        So strange it was that Mosby's men
        Should dare to prowl where the Dome was seen.

A scout toward Aldie broke the spell.—
  The Leader lies before his tent
Gazing at heaven's all-cheering lamp
Through blandness of a morning rare;
  His thoughts on bitter-sweets are bent:
    His sunny bride is in the camp—
    But Mosby—graves are beds of damp!

The trumpet calls; he goes within;
  But none the prayer and sob may know:
Her hero he, but bridegroom too.
Ah, love in a tent is a queenly thing,
  And fame, be sure, refines the vow;
    But fame fond wives have lived to rue,
    And Mosby's men fell deeds can do.

Tan-tara! tan-tara! tan-tara!
  Mounted and armed he sits a king;
For pride she smiles if now she peep—
Elate he rides at the head of his men;
  He is young, and command is a boyish thing:
    They file out into the forest deep—
    Do Mosby and his rangers sleep?

The sun is gold, and the world is green,
  Opal the vapors of morning roll;
The champing horses lightly prance—
Full of caprice, and the riders too
  Curving in many a caricole.
      But marshaled soon, by fours advance—
      Mosby had checked that airy dance.

By the hospital-tent the cripples stand—
  Bandage, and crutch, and cane, and sling,
And palely eye the brave array;
The froth of the cup is gone for them
  (Caw! caw! the crows through the blueness wing):
      Yet these were late as bold, as gay;
      But Mosby—a clip, and grass is hay.

How strong they feel on their horses free,
  Tingles the tendoned thigh with life;
Their cavalry-jackets make boys of all—
With golden breasts like the oriole;
  The chat, the jest, and laugh are rife.
      But word is passed from the front—a call
      For order; the wood is Mosby's hall.

To which behest one rider sly
  (Spurred, but unarmed) gave little heed—
Of dexterous fun not slow or spare,
He teased his neighbors of touchy mood,
   Into plungings he pricked his steed:
     A black-eyed man on a coal-black mare,
     Alive as Mosby in mountain air.

His limbs were long, and large, and round;
  He whispered, winked—did all but shout:
A healthy man for the sick to view;
The taste in his mouth was sweet at morn;
   Little of care he cared about.
     And yet of pains and pangs he knew—
     In others, maimed by Mosby's crew.

The Hospital Steward—even he
  (Sacred in person as a priest),
And on his coat-sleeve broidered nice
Wore the caduceus, black and green.
  No wonder he sat so light on his beast;
     This cheery man in suit of price
     Not even Mosby dared to slice.

They pass the picket by the pine
  And hollow log—a lonesome place;
His horse adroop, and pistol clean;
'Tis cocked—kept leveled toward the wood;
  Strained vigilance ages his childish face.
    Since midnight has that stripling been
    Peering for Mosby through the green.

Splashing they cross the freshet-flood,
  And up the muddy bank they strain;
A horse at a spectral white-ash shies—
One of the span of the ambulance,
  Black as a hearse. They give the rein:
    Silent speed on a scout were wise,
    Could cunning baffle Mosby's spies.

Rumor had come that a band was lodged
  In green retreats of hills that peer
By Aldie (famed for the swordless charge[v]).
Much store they'd heaped of captured arms
  And, peradventure, pilfered cheer;
    For Mosby's lads oft hearts enlarge
    In revelry by some gorge's marge.

"Don't let your sabres rattle and ring;
To his oat-bag let each man give heed—
There now, that fellow's bag's untied,
Sowing the road with the precious grain.
  Your carbines swing at hand—you need!
    Look to yourselves, and your nags beside,
    Men who after Mosby ride."

Picked lads and keen went sharp before—
A guard, though scarce against surprise;
And rearmost rode an answering troop,
But flankers none to right or left.
  No bugle peals, no pennon flies:
    Silent they sweep, and fain would swoop
    On Mosby with an Indian whoop.

On, right on through the forest land,
Nor man, nor maid, nor child was seen—
Not even a dog. The air was still;
The blackened hut they turned to see,
  And spied charred benches on the green;
    A squirrel sprang from the rotting mill
    Whence Mosby sallied late, brave blood to spill.

I

By worn-out fields they cantered on—
   Drear fields amid the woodlands wide;
By cross-roads of some olden time,
In which grew groves; by gate-stones down—
   Grassed ruins of secluded pride:
      A strange lone land, long past the prime,
      Fit land for Mosby or for crime.

The brook in the dell they pass. One peers
   Between the leaves: " Ay, there's the place—
There, on the oozy ledge—'twas there
We found the body (Blake's, you know);
   Such whirlings, gurglings round the face—
      Shot drinking! Well, in war all's fair—
      So Mosby says. The bough—take care!"

Hard by, a chapel. Flower-pot mould
   Danked and decayed the shaded roof;
The porch was punk; the clapboards spanned
With ruffled lichens gray or green;
   Red coral-moss was not aloof;
      And mid dry leaves green dead-man's-hand
      Groped toward that chapel in Mosby-land.

They leave the road and take the wood,
　　And mark the trace of ridges there—
A wood where once had slept the farm—
A wood where once tobacco grew
　　Drowsily in the hazy air,
　　　　And wrought in all kind things a calm—
　　　　Such influence, Mosby! bids disarm.

To ease even yet the place did woo—
　　To ease which pines unstirring share,
For ease the weary horses sighed:
Halting, and slackening girths, they feed,
　　Their pipes they light, they loiter there;
　　　　Then up, and urging still the Guide,
　　　　On, and after Mosby ride.

This Guide in frowzy coat of brown,
　　And beard of ancient growth and mould,
Bestrode a bony steed and strong,
As suited well with bulk he bore—
　　A wheezy man with depth of hold
　　　　Who jouncing went. A staff he swung—
　　　　A wight whom Mosby's wasp had stung.

Burnt out and homeless—hunted long!
  That wheeze he caught in autumn-wood
Crouching (a fat man) for his life,
And spied his lean son 'mong the crew
  That probed the covert. Ah! black blood
    Was his 'gainst even child and wife—
    Fast friends to Mosby. Such the strife.

A lad, unhorsed by sliding girths,
  Strains hard to readjust his seat
Ere the main body show the gap
'Twixt them and the rear-guard; scrub-oaks near
  He sidelong eyes, while hands move fleet;
    Then mounts and spurs. One drops his cap—
    "Let Mosby find!" nor heeds mishap.

A gable time-stained peeps through trees:
  "You mind the fight in the haunted house?
That's it; we clenched them in the room—
An ambuscade of ghosts, we thought,
  But proved sly rebels on a bouse!
    Luke lies in the yard." The chimneys loom:
    Some muse on Mosby—some on doom.

Less nimbly now through brakes they wind,
  And ford wild creeks where men have drowned;
They skirt the pool, avoid the fen,
And so till night, when down they lie,
    Their steeds still saddled, in wooded ground:
      Rein in hand they slumber then,
      Dreaming of Mosby's cedarn den.

But Colonel and Major friendly sat
  Where boughs deformed low made a seat.
The Young Man talked (all sworded and spurred)
Of the partisan's blade he longed to win,
  And frays in which he meant to beat.
      The grizzled Major smoked, and heard:
      "But what's that—Mosby?" "No, a bird."

A contrast here like sire and son,
  Hope and Experience sage did meet;
The Youth was brave, the Senior too;
But through the Seven Days one had served,
  And gasped with the rear-guard in retreat:
      So he smoked and smoked, and the wreath he
        blew—
      "Any *sure* news of Mosby's crew?"

He smoked and smoked, eying the while
  A huge tree hydra-like in growth—
Moon-tinged—with crook'd boughs rent or lopped—
Itself a haggard forest. "Come!"
  The Colonel cried, "to talk you're loath;
      D'ye hear? I say he must be stopped,
      This Mosby—caged, and hair close cropped."

"Of course; but what's that dangling there?"
  "Where?" "From the tree—that gallows-bough;"
"A bit of frayed bark, is it not?"
"Ay—or a rope; did *we* hang last?—
  Don't like my neckerchief any how;"
      He loosened it: "O ay, we'll stop
      This Mosby—but that vile jerk and drop!"

By peep of light they feed and ride,
  Gaining a grove's green edge at morn,
And mark the Aldie hills uprear
And five gigantic horsemen carved
  Clear-cut against the sky withdrawn;
      Are more behind? an open snare?
      Or Mosby's men but watchmen there?

The ravaged land was miles behind,
  And Loudon spread her landscape rare;
Orchards in pleasant lowlands stood,
Cows were feeding, a cock loud crew,
    But not a friend at need was there;
      The valley-folk were only good
        To Mosby and his wandering brood.

What best to do? what mean yon men?
  Colonel and Guide their minds compare;
Be sure some looked their Leader through;
Dismounted, on his sword he leaned
  As one who feigns an easy air;
    And yet perplexed he was they knew—
      Perplexed by Mosby's mountain-crew.

The Major hemmed as he would speak,
  But checked himself, and left the ring
Of cavalrymen about their Chief—
Young courtiers mute who paid their court
  By looking with confidence on their king;
    They knew him brave, foresaw no grief—
      But Mosby—the time to think is brief.

The Surgeon (sashed in sacred green)
　Was glad 'twas not for *him* to say
What next should be; if a trooper bleeds,
Why he will do his best, as wont,
　　And his partner in black will aid and pray;
　　　　But judgment bides with him who leads,
　　　　And Mosby many a problem breeds.

This Surgeon was the kindliest man
　That ever a callous trade professed;
He felt for him, that Leader young,
And offered medicine from his flask:
　　The Colonel took it with marvelous zest.
　　　　For such fine medicine good and strong,
　　　　Oft Mosby and his foresters long.

A charm of proof.　"Ho, Major, come—
　Pounce on yon men!　Take half your troop,
Through the thickets wind—pray speedy be—
And gain their rear.　And, Captain Morn,
　　Picket these roads—all travelers stop;
　　　　The rest to the edge of this crest with me,
　　　　That Mosby and his scouts may see."

Commanded and done. Ere the sun stood steep,
　　Back came the Blues, with a troop of Grays,
Ten riding double—luckless ten!—
Five horses gone, and looped hats lost,
　　And love-locks dancing in a maze—
　　　　Certes, but sophomores from the glen
　　　　Of Mosby—not his veteran men.

"Colonel," said the Major, touching his cap,
　　"We've had our ride, and here they are."
"Well done! how many found you there?"
"As many as I bring you here."
　　"And no one hurt?" "There'll be no scar—
　　　　One fool was battered." "Find their lair?"
　　　　"Why, Mosby's brood camp every where."

He sighed, and slid down from his horse,
　　And limping went to a spring-head nigh.
"Why, bless me, Major, not hurt, I hope?"
"Battered my knee against a bar
　　When the rush was made; all right by-and-by.—
　　　　Halloa! they gave you too much rope—
　　　　Go back to Mosby, eh? elope?"

Just by the low-hanging skirt of wood
  The guard, remiss, had given a chance
For a sudden sally into the cover—
But foiled the intent, nor fired a shot,
  Though the issue was a deadly trance;
      For, hurled 'gainst an oak that humped low over,
      Mosby's man fell, pale as a lover.

They pulled some grass his head to ease
  (Lined with blue shreds a ground-nest stirred).
The Surgeon came—"Here's a to-do!"
"Ah!" cried the Major, darting a glance,
  "This fellow's the one that fired and spurred
      Down hill, but met reserves below—
      My boys, not Mosby's—so we go!"

The Surgeon—bluff, red, goodly man—
  Kneeled by the hurt one; like a bee
He toiled. The pale young Chaplain too—
(Who went to the wars for cure of souls,
  And his own student-ailments)—he
      Bent over likewise; spite the two,
      Mosby's poor man more pallid grew.

Meanwhile the mounted captives near
  Jested; and yet they anxious showed;
Virginians; some of family-pride,
And young, and full of fire, and fine
  In open feature and cheek that glowed;
      And here thralled vagabonds now they ride—
      But list! one speaks for Mosby's side.

"Why, three to one—your horses strong—
  Revolvers, rifles, and a surprise—
Surrender we account no shame!
We live, are gay, and life is hope;
  We'll fight again when fight is wise.
      There are plenty more from where we came;
      But go find Mosby—start the game!"

Yet one there was who looked but glum;
  In middle-age, a father he,
And this his first experience too:
"They shot at my heart when my hands were up—
  This fighting's crazy work, I see!"
      But noon is high; what next to do?
      The woods are mute, and Mosby is the foe.

" Save what we've got," the Major said ;
　" Bad plan to make a scout too long ;
The tide may turn, and drag them back,
And more beside. These rides I've been,
　And every time a mine was sprung.
　　To rescue, mind, they won't be slack—
　　Look out for Mosby's rifle-crack."

" We'll welcome it ! give crack for crack !
　Peril, old lad, is what I seek."
" O then, there's plenty to be had—
By all means on, and have our fill !"
　With that, grotesque, he writhed his neck,
　　Showing a scar by buck-shot made—
　　Kind Mosby's Christmas gift, he said.

" But, Colonel, my prisoners—let a guard
　Make sure of them, and lead to camp.
That done, we're free for a dark-room fight
If so you say." The other laughed ;
　" Trust me, Major, nor throw a damp.
　　But first to try a little sleight—
　　Sure news of Mosby would suit me quite."

Herewith he turned—"Reb, have a dram?"
  Holding the Surgeon's flask with a smile
To a young scapegrace from the glen.
"O yes!" he eagerly replied,
    "And thank you, Colonel, but—any guile?
      For if you think we'll blab—why, then
      You don't know Mosby or his men."

The Leader's genial air relaxed.
  "Best give it up," a whisperer said.
"By heaven, I'll range their rebel den!"
"They'll treat you well," the captive cried;
    "They're all like us—handsome—well bred:
      In wood or town, with sword or pen,
      Polite is Mosby, bland his men."

"Where were you, lads, last night?—come, tell!"
  "We?—at a wedding in the Vale—
The bridegroom our comrade; by his side
Belisent, my cousin—O, so proud
  Of her young love with old wounds pale—
      A Virginian girl! God bless her pride—
      Of a crippled Mosby-man the bride!"

"Four walls shall mend that saucy mood,
　And moping prisons tame him down,"
Said Captain Cloud.　"God help that day,"
Cried Captain Morn, "and he so young.
　But hark, he sings—a madcap one!"
　　"*O we multiply merrily in the May,*
　　The birds and Mosby's men, they say!"

While echoes ran, a wagon old,
　Under stout guard of Corporal Chew
Came up; a lame horse, dingy white,
With clouted harness; ropes in hand,
　Cringed the humped driver, black in hue;
　　By him (for Mosby's band a sight)
　　A sister-rebel sat, her veil held tight.

"I picked them up," the Corporal said,
　"Crunching their way over stick and root,
Through yonder wood.　The man here—Cuff—
Says they are going to Leesburg town."
　The Colonel's eye took in the group;
　　The veiled one's hand he spied—enough!
　　Not Mosby's.　Spite the gown's poor stuff,

Off went his hat: "Lady, fear not;
  We soldiers do what we deplore—
I must detain you till we march."
The stranger nodded. Nettled now,
  He grew politer than before :—
      "'Tis Mosby's fault, this halt and search :"
      The lady stiffened in her starch.

"My duty, madam, bids me now
  Ask what may seem a little rude .
Pardon—that veil—withdraw it, please
(Corporal! make every man fall back);
  Pray, now, I do but what I should ;
      Bethink you, 'tis in masks like these
      That Mosby haunts the villages."

Slowly the stranger drew her veil,
  And looked the Soldier in the eye—
A glance of mingled foul and fair ;
Sad patience in a proud disdain,
  And more than quietude. A sigh
      She heaved, as if all unaware,
      And far seemed Mosby from her care.

She came from Yewton Place, her home,
  So ravaged by the war's wild play—
Campings, and foragings, and fires—
That now she sought an aunt's abode.
    Her kinsmen? In Lee's army, they.
        The black? A servant, late her sire's.
        And Mosby? Vainly he inquires.

He gazed, and sad she met his eye;
  "In the wood yonder were you lost?"
No; at the forks they left the road
Because of hoof-prints (thick they were—
    Thick as the words in notes thrice crossed),
        And fearful, made that episode.
        In fear of Mosby? None she showed.

Her poor attire again he scanned:
  "Lady, once more; I grieve to jar
On all sweet usage, but must plead
To have what peeps there from your dress;
    That letter—'tis justly prize of war."
        She started—gave it—she must need.
        "'Tis not from Mosby? May I read?"

And straight such matter he perused
  That with the Guide he went apart.
The Hospital Steward's turn began:
" Must squeeze this darkey ; every tap
  Of knowledge we are bound to start."
      " Garry," she said, " tell all you can
      Of Colonel Mosby—that brave man."

" Dun know much, sare ; and missis here
  Know less dan me. But dis I know—"
" Well, what ?" " I dun know what I know."
" A knowing answer !" The hump-back coughed,
  Rubbing his yellowish wool like tow.
      " Come—Mosby—tell !" " O dun look so !
      My gal nursed missis—let we go."

" Go where ?" demanded Captain Cloud ;
  " Back into bondage ? Man, you're free !"
" Well, *let* we free !" The Captain's brow
Lowered ; the Colonel came—had heard :
  " Pooh ! pooh ! his simple heart I see—
      A faithful servant.—Lady" (a bow),
      " Mosby's abroad—with us you'll go.

" Guard! look to your prisoners ; back to camp!
   The man in the grass—can he mount and away?
Why, how he groans !"   " Bad inward bruise—
Might lug him along in the ambulance."
   " Coals to Newcastle! let him stay.
         Boots and saddles !—our pains we lose,
         Nor care I if Mosby hear the news !"

But word was sent to a house at hand,
   And a flask was left by the hurt one's side.
They seized in that same house a man,
Neutral by day, by night a foe—
   So charged his neighbor late, the Guide.
         A grudge? Hate will do what it can ;
         Along he went for a Mosby-man.

No secrets now ; the bugle calls ;
   The open road they take, nor shun
The hill ; retrace the weary way.
But one there was who whispered low,
   " This is a feint—we'll back anon ;
         Young Hair-Brains don't retreat, they say ;
         A brush with Mosby is the play !"

They rode till eve.   Then on a farm
  That lay along a hill-side green,
Bivouacked.   Fires were made, and then
Coffee was boiled; a cow was coaxed
    And killed, and savory roasts were seen;
      And under the lee of a cattle-pen
      The guard supped freely with Mosby's men.

The ball was bandied to and fro;
  Hits were given and hits were met:
"Chickamauga, Feds—take off your hat!"
"But the Fight in the Clouds repaid you, Rebs!"
    "Forgotten about Manassas yet?"
      Chatting and chaffing, and tit for tat,
      Mosby's clan with the troopers sat.

"Here comes the moon!" a captive cried;
  "A song! what say? Archy, my lad!"
Hailing the still one of the clan
(A boyish face with girlish hair),
    "Give us that thing poor Pansy made
      Last year."   He brightened, and began;
      And this was the song of Mosby's man:

Spring is come; she shows her pass—
    Wild violets cool!
South of woods a small close grass—
    A vernal wool!
Leaves are a'bud on the sassafras—
    They'll soon be full:
Blessings on the friendly screen—
I'm for the South! says the leafage green.

Robins! fly, and take your fill
    Of out-of-doors—
Garden, orchard, meadow, hill,
    Barns and bowers;
Take your fill, and have your will—
    Virginia's yours!
But, bluebirds! keep away, and fear
The ambuscade in bushes here.

"A green song that," a sergeant said;
    "But where's poor Pansy? gone, I fear."
"Ay, mustered out at Ashby's Gap."
"I see; now for a live man's song;
    Ditty for ditty—prepare to cheer.
        My bluebirds, you can fling a cap!
        You barehead Mosby-boys—why—clap!"

Nine Blue-coats went a-nutting
　　Slyly in Tennessee—
Not for chestnuts—better than that—
　　Hush, you bumble-bee !
　　　Nutting, nutting—
　　All through the year there's nutting !

A tree they spied so yellow,
　　Rustling in motion queer ;
In they fired, and down they dropped—
　　Butternuts, my dear !
　　　Nutting, nutting—
　　Who'll 'list to go a-nutting ?

Ah! why should good fellows foemen be?
　And who would dream that foes they were—
Larking and singing so friendly then—
A family likeness in every face.
　But Captain Cloud made sour demur :
　　"Guard! keep your prisoners *in* the pen,
　　And let none talk with Mosby's men."

That captain was a valorous one
  (No irony, but honest truth),
Yet down from his brain cold drops distilled,
Making stalactites in his heart—
    A conscientious soul, forsooth;
        And with a formal hate was filled
        Of Mosby's band; and some he'd killed.

Meantime the lady rueful sat,
  Watching the flicker of a fire
Where the Colonel played the outdoor host
In brave old hall of ancient Night.
    But ever the dame grew shyer and shyer,
        Seeming with private grief engrossed—
        Grief far from Mosby, housed or lost.

The ruddy embers showed her pale.
  The Soldier did his best devoir:
" Some coffee?—no?—a cracker?—one?"
Cared for her servant—sought to cheer:
  " I know, I know—a cruel war!
      But wait—even Mosby 'll eat his bun;
      The Old Hearth—back to it anon!"

But cordial words no balm could bring;
  She sighed, and kept her inward chafe,
And seemed to hate the voice of glee—
Joyless and tearless. Soon he called
    An escort: "See this lady safe
      In yonder house.—Madam, you're free.
      And now for Mosby.—Guide! with me."

("A night-ride, eh?") "Tighten your girths!
  But, buglers! not a note from you.
Fling more rails on the fires—a blaze!"
("Sergeant, a feint—I told you so—
  Toward Aldie again. Bivouac, adieu!")
      After the cheery flames they gaze,
      Then back for Mosby through the maze.

The moon looked through the trees, and tipped
  The scabbards with her elfin beam;
The Leader backward cast his glance,
Proud of the cavalcade that came—
  A hundred horses, bay and cream:
      "Major! look how the lads advance—
      Mosby we'll have in the ambulance!"

"No doubt, no doubt :—was that a hare?—
  First catch, then cook; and cook him brown."
"Trust me to catch," the other cried—
"The lady's letter!—a dance, man, dance
  This night is given in Leesburg town!"
      "He'll be there too!" wheezed out the Guide;
      "That Mosby loves a dance and ride!"

"The lady, ah!—the lady's letter—
  A *lady*, then, is in the case,"
Muttered the Major.   "Ay, her aunt
Writes her to come by Friday eve
  (To-night), for people of the place,
      At Mosby's last fight jubilant,
      A party give, though table-cheer be scant."

The Major hemmed.   "Then this night-ride
  We owe to her?—One lighted house
In a town else dark.—The moths, begar!
Are not quite yet all dead!"   "How? how?"
  "A mute, meek, mournful little mouse!—
      Mosby has wiles which subtle are—
      But woman's wiles in wiles of war!"

"Tut, Major! by what craft or guile—"
"Can't tell! but he'll be found in wait.
Softly we enter, say, the town—
Good! pickets post, and all so sure—
   When—crack! the rifles from every gate,
      The Gray-backs fire—dash up and down—
      Each alley unto Mosby known!"

"Now, Major, now—you take dark views
   Of a moonlight night." "Well, well, we'll see,"
And smoked as if each whiff were gain.
The other mused; then sudden asked,
   "What would you do in grand decree?"
      "I'd beat, if I could, Lee's armies—then
      Send constables after Mosby's men."

"Ay! ay!—you're odd." The moon sailed up;
   On through the shadowy land they went.
"*Names must be made and printed be!*"
Hummed the blithe Colonel. "Doc, your flask!
   Major, I drink to your good content.
      My pipe is out—enough for me!
      One's buttons shine—does Mosby see?

K

"But what comes here?"   A man from the front
　Reported a tree athwart the road.
"Go round it, then; no time to bide;
All right—go on! Were one to stay
　For each distrust of a nervous mood,
　　　Long miles we'd make in this our ride
　　　Through Mosby-land.—On! with the Guide!"

Then sportful to the Surgeon turned:
　"Green sashes hardly serve by night!"
"Nor bullets nor bottles," the Major sighed,
"Against these moccasin-snakes—such foes
　As seldom come to solid fight:
　　　They kill and vanish; through grass they glide;
　　　Devil take Mosby!"—his horse here shied.

"Hold! look—the tree, like a dragged balloon;
　A globe of leaves—some trickery here;
My nag is right—best now be shy."
A movement was made, a hubbub and snarl;
　Little was plain—they blindly steer.
　　　The Pleiads, as from ambush sly,
　　　Peep out—Mosby's men in the sky!

As restive they turn, how sore they feel,
  And cross, and sleepy, and full of spleen,
And curse the war. "Fools, North and South!"
Said one right out. "O for a bed!
  O now to drop in this woodland green!"
      He drops as the syllables leave his mouth—
      Mosby speaks from the undergrowth—

Speaks in a volley! out jets the flame!
  Men fall from their saddles like plums from trees;
Horses take fright, reins tangle and bind;
"Steady—dismount—form—and into the wood!"
  They go, but find what scarce can please:
      Their steeds have been tied in the field behind,
      And Mosby's men are off like the wind.

Sound the recall! vain to pursue—
  The enemy scatters in wilds he knows,
To reunite in his own good time;
And, to follow, they need divide—
  To come lone and lost on crouching foes:
      Maple and hemlock, beech and lime,
      Are Mosby's confederates, share the crime.

"Major," burst in a bugler small,
  "The fellow we left in Loudon grass—
Sir Slyboots with the inward bruise,
His voice I heard—the very same—
  Some watchword in the ambush pass;
    Ay, sir, we had him in his shoes—
    We caught him—Mosby—but to lose!"

"Go, go!—these saddle-dreamers! Well,
  And here's another.—Cool, sir, cool!"
"Major, I saw them mount and sweep,
And one was humped, or I mistake,
  And in the skurry dropped his wool."
    "A wig! go fetch it:—the lads need sleep;
    They'll next see Mosby in a sheep!

"Come, come, fall back! reform your ranks—
  All's jackstraws here! Where's Captain Morn?—
We've parted like boats in a raging tide!
But stay—the Colonel—did he charge?
  And comes he there? 'Tis streak of dawn;
    Mosby is off, the woods are wide—
    Hist! there's a groan—this crazy ride!"

As they searched for the fallen, the dawn grew chill;
  They lay in the dew: "Ah! hurt much, Mink?
And—yes—the Colonel!" Dead! but so calm
That death seemed nothing—even death,
  The thing we deem every thing heart can think;
    Amid wilding roses that shed their balm,
    Careless of Mosby he lay—in a charm!

The Major took him by the hand—
  Into the friendly clasp it bled
(A ball through heart and hand he rued):
"Good-by!" and gazed with humid glance;
  Then in a hollow revery said,
    "The weakest thing is lustihood;
    But Mosby"—and he checked his mood.

"Where's the advance?—cut off, by heaven!
  Come, Surgeon, how with your wounded there?"
"The ambulance will carry all."
"Well, get them in; we go to camp.
  Seven prisoners gone? for the rest have care."
    Then to himself, "This grief is gall;
    That Mosby!—I'll cast a silver ball!"

"Ho!" turning—"Captain Cloud, you mind
    The place where the escort went—so shady?
Go, search every closet low and high,
And barn, and bin, and hidden bower—
    Every covert—find that lady!
        And yet I may misjudge her—ay,
        Women (like Mosby) mystify.

"We'll see.   Ay, Captain, go—with speed!
    Surround and search; each living thing
Secure; that done, await us where
We last turned off.   Stay! fire the cage
    'If the birds be flown."   By the cross-road spring
        The bands rejoined; no words; the glare
        Told all.   Had Mosby plotted there?

The weary troop that wended now—
    Hardly it seemed the same that pricked
Forth to the forest from the camp:
Foot-sore horses, jaded men;
    Every backbone felt as nicked,
        Each eye dim as a sick-room lamp,
        All faces stamped with Mosby's stamp.

In order due the Major rode—
  Chaplain and Surgeon on either hand;
A riderless horse a negro led;
In a wagon the blanketed sleeper went;
  Then the ambulance with the bleeding band;
    And, an emptied oat-bag on each head,
    Went Mosby's men, and marked the dead.

What gloomed them? what so cast them down,
  And changed the cheer that late they took,
As double-guarded now they rode
Between the files of moody men?
  Some sudden consciousness they brook,
    Or dread the sequel. That night's blood
    Disturbed even Mosby's brotherhood.

The flagging horses stumbled at roots,
  Floundered in mires, or clinked the stones;
No rider spake except aside;
But the wounded cramped in the ambulance,
  It was horror to hear their groans—
    Jerked along in the woodland ride,
    While Mosby's clan their revery hide.

The Hospital Steward—even he—
　　Who on the sleeper kept his glance,
Was changed; late bright-black beard and eye
Looked now hearse-black; his heavy heart,
　　Like his fagged mare, no more could dance;
　　　　His grape was now a raisin dry:
　　　　'Tis Mosby's homily—*Man must die.*

The amber sunset flushed the camp
　　As on the hill their eyes they fed;
The pickets dumb looks at the wagon dart;
A handkerchief waves from the bannered tent—
　　As white, alas! the face of the dead:
　　　　Who shall the withering news impart?
　　　　The bullet of Mosby goes through heart to heart!

They buried him where the lone ones lie
　　(Lone sentries shot on midnight post)—
A green-wood grave-yard hid from ken,
Where sweet-fern flings an odor nigh—
　　Yet held in fear for the gleaming ghost!
　　　　Though the bride should see threescore and ten,
　　　　She will dream of Mosby and his men.

Now halt the verse, and turn aside—
    The cypress falls athwart the way;
No joy remains for bard to sing;
And heaviest dole of all is this,
    That other hearts shall be as gay
        As hers that now no more shall spring:
        To Mosby-land the dirges cling.

K 2

LEE IN THE CAPITOL.

Lee in the Capitol.[x]
(April, 1866.)

Hard pressed by numbers in his strait,
   Rebellion's soldier-chief no more contends—
Feels that the hour is come of Fate,
   Lays down one sword, and widened warfare ends.
The captain who fierce armies led
Becomes a quiet seminary's head—
Poor as his privates, earns his bread.
In studious cares and aims engrossed,
   Strives to forget Stuart and Stonewall dead—
Comrades and cause, station and riches lost,
   And all the ills that flock when fortune's fled.
No word he breathes of vain lament,
   Mute to reproach, nor hears applause—
His doom accepts, perforce content,
   And acquiesces in asserted laws;
Secluded now would pass his life,
And leave to time the sequel of the strife.

But missives from the Senators ran ;
Not that they now would gaze upon a swordless foe,
And power made powerless and brought low:
   Reasons of state, 'tis claimed, require the man.
Demurring not, promptly he comes
By ways which show the blackened homes,
   And—last—the seat no more his own,
But Honor's ; patriot grave-yards fill
The forfeit slopes of that patrician hill,
   And fling a shroud on Arlington.
The oaks ancestral all are low ;
No more from the porch his glance shall go
Ranging the varied landscape o'er,
Far as the looming Dome—no more.
One look he gives, then turns aside,
Solace he summons from his pride:
" So be it ! They await me now
Who wrought this stinging overthrow ;
They wait me ; not as on the day
Of Pope's impelled retreat in disarray—
By me impelled—when toward yon Dome
The clouds of war came rolling home."
The burst, the bitterness was spent,
The heart-burst bitterly turbulent,
And on he fared.

In nearness now
He marks the Capitol—a show
Lifted in amplitude, and set
With standards flushed with the glow of Richmond yet;
Trees and green terraces sleep below.
Through the clear air, in sunny light,
The marble dazes—a temple white.

Intrepid soldier! had his blade been drawn
For yon starred flag, never as now
Bid to the Senate-house had he gone,
But freely, and in pageant borne,
As when brave numbers without number, massed,
Plumed the broad way, and pouring passed—
Bannered, beflowered—between the shores
Of faces, and the dinn'd huzzas,
And balconies kindling at the sabre-flash,
'Mid roar of drums and guns, and cymbal-crash,
While Grant and Sherman shone in blue—
Close of the war and victory's long review.

Yet pride at hand still aidful swelled,
And up the hard ascent he held.
The meeting follows. In his mien
The victor and the vanquished both are seen—
All that he is, and what he late had been.

Awhile, with curious eyes they scan
The Chief who led invasion's van—
Allied by family to one,
Founder of the Arch the Invader warred upon:
Who looks at Lee must think of Washington;
In pain must think, and hide the thought,
So deep with grievous meaning it is fraught.

Secession in her soldier shows
Silent and patient; and they feel
   (Developed even in just success)
Dim inklings of a hazy future steal;
   Their thoughts their questions well express:
"Does the sad South still cherish hate?
Freely will Southern men with Northern mate?
The blacks—should we our arm withdraw,
Would that betray them? some distrust your law.
And how if foreign fleets should come—
Would the South then drive her wedges home?"
And more hereof. The Virginian sees—
Replies to such anxieties.
Discreet his answers run—appear
Briefly straightforward, coldly clear.

" If now," the Senators, closing, say,
" Aught else remain, speak out, we pray."

Hereat he paused; his better heart
Strove strongly then; prompted a worthier part
Than coldly to endure his doom.
Speak out? Ay, speak, and for the brave,
Who else no voice or proxy have;
Frankly their spokesman here become,
And the flushed North from her own victory save.
That inspiration overrode—
Hardly it quelled the galling load
Of personal ill. The inner feud
He, self-contained, a while withstood;
They waiting. In his troubled eye
Shadows from clouds unseen they spy;
They could not mark within his breast
The pang which pleading thought oppressed :
He spoke, nor felt the bitterness die.

"My word is given—it ties my sword;
Even were banners still abroad,
Never could I strive in arms again
While you, as fit, that pledge retain.
Our cause I followed, stood in field and gate—
All's over now, and now I follow Fate.
But this is naught. A People call—
A desolated land, and all

The brood of ills that press so sore,
The natural offspring of this civil war,
Which ending not in fame, such as might rear
Fitly its sculptured trophy here,
Yields harvest large of doubt and dread
To all who have the heart and head
To feel and know.   How shall I speak?
Thoughts knot with thoughts, and utterance check.
Before my eyes there swims a haze,
Through mists departed comrades gaze—
First to encourage, last that shall upbraid!
How shall I speak?   The South would fain
Feel peace, have quiet law again—
Replant the trees for homestead-shade.

    You ask if she recants: she yields.
Nay, and would more; would blend anew,
As the bones of the slain in her forests do,
Bewailed alike by us and you.

    A voice comes out from these charnel-fields,
A plaintive yet unheeded one:
'*Died all in vain? both sides undone?*'
Push not your triumph; do not urge
Submissiveness beyond the verge.
Intestine rancor would you bide,
Nursing eleven sliding daggers in your side?

Far from my thought to school or threat;
I speak the things which hard beset.
Where various hazards meet the eyes,
To elect in magnanimity is wise.
Reap victory's fruit while sound the core;
What sounder fruit than re-established law?
I know your partial thoughts do press
Solely on us for war's unhappy stress;
But weigh—consider—look at all,
And broad anathema you'll recall.
The censor's charge I'll not repeat,
That meddlers kindled the war's white heat—
Vain intermeddlers and malign,
Both of the palm and of the pine;
I waive the thought—which never can be rife—
Common's the crime in every civil strife:
But this I feel, that North and South were driven
By Fate to arms. For *our* unshriven,
What thousands, truest souls, were tried—
　　As never may any be again—
All those who stemmed Secession's pride,
But at last were swept by the urgent tide
　　Into the chasm. I know their pain.
A story here may be applied:
'In Moorish lands there lived a maid
　　Brought to confess by vow the creed

Of Christians. Fain would priests persuade
That now she must approve by deed
 The faith she kept. "What deed?" she asked.
"Your old sire leave, nor deem it sin,
 And come with us." Still more they tasked
The sad one: "If heaven you'd win—
 Far from the burning pit withdraw,
Then must you learn to hate your kin,
 Yea, side against them—such the law,
For Moor and Christian are at war."
"Then will I never quit my sire,
But here with him through every trial go,
Nor leave him though in flames below—
God help me in his fire!"'
So in the South; vain every plea
'Gainst Nature's strong fidelity;
 True to the home and to the heart,
Throngs cast their lot with kith and kin,
 Foreboding, cleaved to the natural part—
Was this the unforgivable sin?
These noble spirits are yet yours to win.
Shall the great North go Sylla's way?
Proscribe? prolong the evil day?
Confirm the curse? infix the hate?
In Union's name forever alienate?

From reason who can urge the plea—
Freemen conquerors of the free?
When blood returns to the shrunken vein,
Shall the wound of the Nation bleed again?
Well may the wars wan thought supply,
And kill the kindling of the hopeful eye,
Unless you do what even kings have done
In leniency—unless you shun
To copy Europe in her worst estate—
Avoid the tyranny you reprobate."

He ceased. His earnestness unforeseen
Moved, but not swayed their former mien;
   And they dismissed him. Forth he went
Through vaulted walks in lengthened line
Like porches erst upon the Palatine:
   Historic reveries their lesson lent,
   The Past her shadow through the Future sent.

But no. Brave though the Soldier, grave his plea—
   Catching the light in the future's skies,
Instinct disowns each darkening prophecy:
   Faith in America never dies;
Heaven shall the end ordained fulfill,
We march with Providence cheery still.

A MEDITATION:

ATTRIBUTED TO A NORTHERNER AFTER ATTENDING THE
LAST OF TWO FUNERALS FROM THE SAME HOMESTEAD—
THOSE OF A NATIONAL AND A CONFEDERATE OFFICER
(BROTHERS), HIS KINSMEN, WHO HAD DIED FROM THE EF-
FECTS OF WOUNDS RECEIVED IN THE CLOSING BATTLES.

A Meditation.

How often in the years that close,
  When truce had stilled the sieging gun,
The soldiers, mounting on their works,
  With mutual curious glance have run
From face to face along the fronting show,
And kinsman spied, or friend—even in a foe.

What thoughts conflicting then were shared,
  While sacred tenderness perforce
Welled from the heart and wet the eye;
  And something of a strange remorse
Rebelled against the sanctioned sin of blood,
And Christian wars of natural brotherhood.

Then stirred the god within the breast—
  The witness that is man's at birth;
A deep misgiving undermined
  Each plea and subterfuge of earth;
They felt in that rapt pause, with warning rife,
Horror and anguish for the civil strife.

L

Of North or South they recked not then,
  Warm passion cursed the cause of war :
Can Africa pay back this blood
  Spilt on Potomac's shore ?
Yet doubts, as pangs, were vain the strife to stay,
And hands that fain had clasped again could slay.

How frequent in the camp was seen
  The herald from the hostile one,
A guest and frank companion there
  When the proud formal talk was done ;
The pipe of peace was smoked even 'mid the war,
And fields in Mexico again fought o'er.

In Western battle long they lay
  So near opposed in trench or pit,
That foeman unto foeman called
  As men who screened in tavern sit :
" You bravely fight" each to the other said—
" Toss us a biscuit !" o'er the wall it sped.

And pale on those same slopes, a boy—
  A stormer, bled in noon-day glare ;
No aid the Blue-coats then could bring,
  He cried to them who nearest were,
And out there came 'mid howling shot and shell
A daring foe who him befriended well.

Mark the great Captains on both sides,
    The soldiers with the broad renown—
They all were messmates on the Hudson's marge,
    Beneath one roof they laid them down;
And, free from hate in many an after pass,
Strove as in school-boy rivalry of the class.

A darker side there is; but doubt
    In Nature's charity hovers there:
If men for new agreement yearn,
    Then old upbraiding best forbear:
"*The South's the sinner!*" Well, so let it be;
But shall the North sin worse, and stand the Pharisee?

O, now that brave men yield the sword,
    Mine be the manful soldier-view;
By how much more they boldly warred,
    By so much more is mercy due:
When Vicksburg fell, and the moody files marched out,
Silent the victors stood, scorning to raise a shout.

N O T E S.

NOTES.

The gloomy lull of the early part of the winter of 1860-1, seeming big with final disaster to our institutions, affected some minds that believed them to constitute one of the great hopes of mankind, much as the eclipse which came over the promise of the first French Revolution affected kindred natures, throwing them for the time into doubts and misgivings universal.

"The terrible Stone Fleet, on a mission as pitiless as the granite that freights it, sailed this morning from Port Royal, and before two days are past will have made Charleston an inland city. The ships are all old whalers, and cost the government from $2500 to $5000 each. Some of them were once famous ships."
—(From Newspaper Correspondence of the day.)

Sixteen vessels were accordingly sunk on the bar at the river entrance. Their names were as follows :

Amazon,	Leonidas,
America,	Maria Theresa,
American,	Potomac,
Archer,	Rebecca Simms,
Courier,	L. C. Richmond,
Fortune,	Robin Hood,
Herald,	Tenedos,
Kensington,	William Lee.

All accounts seem to agree that the object proposed was not accomplished. The channel is even said to have become ultimately benefited by the means employed to obstruct it.

NOTE ^c, *page* 58.

The *Temeraire*, that storied ship of the old English fleet, and the subject of the well-known painting by Turner, commends itself to the mind seeking for some one craft to stand for the poetic ideal of those great historic wooden warships, whose gradual displacement is lamented by none more than by regularly educated navy officers, and of all nations.

NOTE ^d, *page* 59.

Some of the cannon of old times, especially the brass ones, unlike the more effective ordnance of the present day, were cast in shapes which Cellini might have designed, were gracefully enchased, generally with the arms of the country. A few of them—field-pieces—captured in our earlier wars, are preserved in arsenals and navy-yards.

NOTE ^e, *page* 69.

Whatever just military criticism, favorable or otherwise, has at any time been made upon General McClellan's campaigns, will stand.   But if, during the excitement of the conflict, aught was spread abroad tending to unmerited disparagement of the man, it must necessarily die out, though not perhaps without leaving some traces, which may or may not prove enduring.   Some there are whose votes aided in the re-election of Abraham Lincoln, who yet believed, and retain the belief, that General McClellan, to say the least, always proved himself a patriotic and honorable soldier.   The feeling which surviving comrades entertain for their late commander is one which, from its passion, is susceptible of versified representation, and such it receives.

NOTE ^f, *page* 71.

At Antietam Stonewall Jackson led one wing of Lee's army, consequently sharing that day in whatever may be deemed to have been the fortunes of his superior.

NOTE ^g, *page* 78.

Admiral Porter is a son of the late Commodore Porter, commander of the frigate Essex on that Pacific cruise which ended in the desperate fight off Valparaiso with the English frigates Cherub and Phœbe, in the year 1814.

NOTE ^h, *page* 85.

Among numerous head-stones or monuments on Cemetery Hill, marred or destroyed by the enemy's concentrated fire, was one, somewhat conspicuous, of a Federal officer killed before Richmond in 1862.

On the 4th of July, 1865, the Gettysburg National Cemetery, on the same height with the original burial-ground, was consecrated, and the corner-stone laid of a commemorative pile.

NOTE ⁱ, *page* 86.

"I dare not write the horrible and inconceivable atrocities committed," says Froissart, in alluding to the remarkable sedition in France during his time. The like may be hinted of some proceedings of the draft-rioters.

NOTE ^j, *page* 90.

Although the month was November, the day was in character an October one — cool, clear, bright, intoxicatingly invigorating ; one of those days peculiar to the ripest hours of our American autumn. This weather must have had much to do with the spontaneous enthusiasm which seized the troops—an enthusiasm aided, doubtless, by glad thoughts of the victory of Look-out Mountain won the day previous, and also by the elation attending the capture, after a fierce struggle, of the long ranges of rifle-pits at the mountain's base, where orders for the time should have stopped the advance. But there and then it was that the army took the bit between its teeth, and ran away with the generals to the victory commemorated. General Grant, at Culpepper, a few weeks prior to crossing the Rapidan for the Wilderness, expressed to a visitor his impression of the impulse and the spectacle : Said he, "I never saw any thing like it :"

language which seems curiously undertoned, considering its application; but from the taciturn Commander it was equivalent to a superlative or hyperbole from the talkative.

The height of the Ridge, according to the account at hand, varies along its length from six to seven hundred feet above the plain; it slopes at an angle of about forty-five degrees.

NOTE ᵏ, *page* 107.

The great Parrott gun, planted in the marshes of James Island, and employed in the prolonged, though at times intermitted bombardment of Charleston, was known among our soldiers as the Swamp Angel.

St. Michael's, characterized by its venerable tower, was the historic and aristocratic church of the town.

NOTE ˡ, *page* 122.

Among the Northwestern regiments there would seem to have been more than one which carried a living eagle as an added ensign. The bird commemorated here was, according to the account, borne aloft on a perch beside the standard; went through successive battles and campaigns; was more than once under the surgeon's hands; and at the close of the contest found honorable repose in the capital of Wisconsin, from which state he had gone to the wars.

NOTE ᵐ, *page* 124.

The late Major General McPherson, commanding the Army of the Tennessee, a native of Ohio and a West Pointer, was one of the foremost spirits of the war. Young, though a veteran; hardy, intrepid, sensitive in honor, full of engaging qualities, with manly beauty; possessed of genius, a favorite with the army, and with Grant and Sherman. Both Generals have generously acknowledged their professional obligations to the able engineer and admirable soldier, their subordinate and junior.

In an informal account written by the Achilles to this Sarpedon, he says:

"On that day we avenged his death. Near twenty-two hundred of the enemy's dead remained on the ground when night closed upon the scene of action."

It is significant of the scale on which the war was waged, that the engagement thus written of goes solely (so far as can be learned) under the vague designation of one of the battles before Atlanta.

NOTE ⁿ, *page* 133.

This piece was written while yet the reports were coming North of Sherman's homeward advance from Savannah. It is needless to point out its purely dramatic character.

Though the sentiment ascribed in the beginning of the second stanza must, in the present reading, suggest the historic tragedy of the 14th of April, nevertheless, as intimated, it was written prior to that event, and without any distinct application in the writer's mind. After consideration, it is allowed to remain.

Few need be reminded that, by the less intelligent classes of the South, Abraham Lincoln, by nature the most kindly of men, was regarded as a monster wantonly warring upon liberty. He stood for the personification of tyrannic power. Each Union soldier was called a Lincolnite.

Undoubtedly Sherman, in the desolation he inflicted after leaving Atlanta, acted not in contravention of orders; and all, in a military point of view, is by military judges deemed to have been expedient, and nothing can abate General Sherman's shining renown; his claims to it rest on no single campaign. Still, there are those who can not but contrast some of the scenes enacted in Georgia and the Carolinas, and also in the Shenandoah, with a circumstance in a great Civil War of heathen antiquity. Plutarch relates that in a military council held by Pompey and the chiefs of that party which stood for the Commonwealth, it was decided that under no plea should any city be sacked that was subject to the people of Rome. There was this difference, however, between the Roman civil conflict and the American one. The war of Pompey and Cæsar divided the Roman people promiscuously; that of the North and South ran a frontier line between what for the time were distinct communities or nations. In this circumstance, possibly, and some others, may be found both the cause and the justification of some of the sweeping measures adopted.

Note [o], *page* 142.

At this period of excitement the thought was by some passionately welcomed that the Presidential successor had been raised up by heaven to wreak vengeance on the South. The idea originated in the remembrance that Andrew Johnson by birth belonged to that class of Southern whites who never cherished love for the dominant one; that he was a citizen of Tennessee, where the contest at times and in places had been close and bitter as a Middle-Age feud; that himself and family had been hardly treated by the Secessionists.

But the expectations built hereon (if, indeed, ever soberly entertained), happily for the country, have not been verified.

Likewise the feeling which would have held the entire South chargeable with the crime of one exceptional assassin, this too has died away with the natural excitement of the hour.

Note [p], *page* 144.

The incident on which this piece is based is narrated in a newspaper account of the battle to be found in the "Rebellion Record." During the disaster to the national forces on the first day, a brigade on the extreme left found itself isolated. The perils it encountered are given in detail. Among others, the following sentences occur:

"Under cover of the fire from the bluffs, the rebels rushed down, crossed the ford, and in a moment were seen forming this side the creek in open fields, and within close musket-range. Their color-bearers stepped defiantly to the front as the engagement opened furiously; the rebels pouring in sharp, quick volleys of musketry, and their batteries above continuing to support them with a destructive fire. Our sharpshooters wanted to pick off the audacious rebel color-bearers, but Colonel Stuart interposed: "No, no, they're too brave fellows to be killed."

Note [q], *page* 146.

According to a report of the Secretary of War, there were on the first day of March, 1865, 965,000 men on the army pay-rolls. Of these, some 200,000—

artillery, cavalry, and infantry—made up from the larger portion of the veterans of Grant and Sherman, marched by the President. The total number of Union troops enlisted during the war was 2,668,000.

NOTE ᶦ, *page* 150.

For a month or two after the completion of peace, some thousands of released captives from the military prisons of the North, natives of all parts of the South, passed through the city of New York, sometimes waiting farther transportation for days, during which interval they wandered penniless about the streets, or lay in their worn and patched gray uniforms under the trees of the Battery, near the barracks where they were lodged and fed. They were transported and provided for at the charge of government.

NOTE ˢ, *page* 153.

Shortly prior to the evacuation of Petersburg, the enemy, with a view to ultimate repossession, interred some of his heavy guns in the same field with his dead, and with every circumstance calculated to deceive. Subsequently the negroes exposed the stratagem.

NOTE ᵗ, *page* 157.

The records of Northern colleges attest what numbers of our noblest youth went from them to the battle-field. Southern members of the same classes arrayed themselves on the side of Secession ; while Southern seminaries contributed large quotas. Of all these, what numbers marched who never returned except on the shield.

NOTE ᵘ, *page* 178.

Written prior to the founding of the National Cemetery at Andersonville, where 15,000 of the reinterred captives now sleep, each beneath his personal head-board, inscribed from records found in the prison-hospital. Some hundreds rest apart and without name. A glance at the published pamphlet containing the list of the buried at Andersonville conveys a feeling mournfully impressive. Seventy-four large double-columned pages in fine print. Looking through them is like getting lost among the old turbaned head-stones and cypresses in the interminable Black Forest of Scutari, over against Constantinople.

NOTE ^v, *page* 192.

In one of Kilpatrick's earlier cavalry fights near Aldie, a Colonel who, being under arrest, had been temporarily deprived of his sword, nevertheless, unarmed, insisted upon charging at the head of his men, which he did, and the onset proved victorious.

NOTE ^w, *page* 198.

Certain of Mosby's followers, on the charge of being unlicensed foragers or fighters, being hung by order of a Union cavalry commander, the Partisan promptly retaliated in the woods. In turn, this also was retaliated, it is said. To what extent such deplorable proceedings were carried, it is not easy to learn.

South of the Potomac in Virginia, and within a gallop of the Long Bridge at Washington, is the confine of a country, in some places wild, which throughout the war it was unsafe for a Union man to traverse except with an armed escort. This was the chase of Mosby, the scene of many of his exploits or those of his men. In the heart of this region at least one fortified camp was maintained by our cavalry, and from time to time expeditions were made therefrom. Owing to the nature of the country and the embittered feeling of its inhabitants, many of these expeditions ended disastrously. Such results were helped by the exceeding cunning of the enemy, born of his wood-craft, and, in some instances, by undue confidence on the part of our men. A body of cavalry, starting from camp with the view of breaking up a nest of rangers, and absent say three days, would return with a number of their own forces killed and wounded (ambushed), without being able to retaliate farther than by foraging on the country, destroying a house or two reported to be haunts of the guerrillas, or capturing non-combatants accused of being secretly active in their behalf.

In the verse the name of Mosby is invested with some of those associations with which the popular mind is familiar. But facts do not warrant the belief that every clandestine attack of men who passed for Mosby's was made under his eye, or even by his knowledge.

In partisan warfare he proved himself shrewd, able, and enterprising, and always a wary fighter. He stood well in the confidence of his superior officers, and was employed by them at times in furtherance of important movements. To our wounded on more than one occasion he showed considerate kindness. Officers and civilians captured by forces under his immediate command were, so long as remaining under his orders, treated with civility. These things are well known to those personally familiar with the irregular fighting in Virginia.

NOTE ˣ, *page* 229.

Among those summoned during the spring just passed to appear before the Reconstruction Committee of Congress was Robert E. Lee. His testimony is deeply interesting, both in itself and as coming from him. After various questions had been put and briefly answered, these words were addressed to him:

"If there be any other matter about which you wish to speak on this occasion, do so freely." Waiving this invitation, he responded by a short personal explanation of some point in a previous answer, and, after a few more brief questions and replies, the interview closed.

In the verse a poetical liberty has been ventured. Lee is not only represented as responding to the invitation, but also as at last renouncing his cold reserve, doubtless the cloak to feelings more or less poignant. If for such freedom warrant be necessary, the speeches in ancient histories, not to speak of those in Shakspeare's historic plays, may not unfitly perhaps be cited.

The character of the original measures proposed about this time in the National Legislature for the treatment of the (as yet) Congressionally excluded South, and the spirit in which those measures were advocated—these are circumstances which it is fairly supposable would have deeply influenced the thoughts, whether spoken or withheld, of a Southerner placed in the position of Lee before the Reconstruction Committee.

S U P P L E M E N T.

WERE I fastidiously anxious for the symmetry of this book, it would close with the notes. But the times are such that patriotism—not free from solicitude—urges a claim overriding all literary scruples.

It is more than a year since the memorable surrender, but events have not yet rounded themselves into completion. Not justly can we complain of this. There has been an upheaval affecting the basis of things; to altered circumstances complicated adaptations are to be made; there are difficulties great and novel. But is Reason still waiting for Passion to spend itself? We have sung of the soldiers and sailors, but who shall hymn the politicians?

In view of the infinite desirableness of Re-establishment, and considering that, so far as feeling is concerned, it depends not mainly on the temper in which the South regards the North, but rather conversely; one who never was a blind adherent feels constrained to submit some thoughts, counting on the indulgence of his countrymen.

And, first, it may be said that, if among the feelings and opinions growing immediately out of a great civil convulsion, there are any which time shall modify or do away, they are presumably those of a less temperate and charitable cast.

There seems no reason why patriotism and narrowness should go together, or why intellectual impartiality should be confounded with political trimming, or why serviceable truth should keep cloistered because not partisan. Yet the work of Reconstruction, if admitted to be feasible at all, demands little but common sense and Christian charity. Little but these? These are much.

Some of us are concerned because as yet the South shows no penitence. But what exactly do we mean by this? Since down to the close of the war she never confessed any for braving it, the only penitence now left her is that which springs solely from the sense of discomfiture; and since this evidently would be a contrition hypocritical, it would be unworthy in us to demand it. Certain it is that penitence, in the sense of voluntary humiliation, will never be displayed. Nor does this afford just ground for unreserved condemnation. It is enough, for all practical purposes, if the South have been taught by the terrors of civil war to feel that Secession, like Slavery, is against Destiny; that both now lie buried in one grave; that her fate is linked with ours; and that together we comprise the Nation.

The clouds of heroes who battled for the Union it is

needless to eulogize here. But how of the soldiers on the other side? And when of a free community we name the soldiers, we thereby name the people. It was in subserviency to the slave-interest that Secession was plotted; but it was under the plea, plausibly urged, that certain inestimable rights guaranteed by the Constitution were directly menaced, that the people of the South were cajoled into revolution. Through the arts of the conspirators and the perversity of fortune, the most sensitive love of liberty was entrapped into the support of a war whose implied end was the erecting in our advanced century of an Anglo-American empire based upon the systematic degradation of man.

Spite this clinging reproach, however, signal military virtues and achievements have conferred upon the Confederate arms historic fame, and upon certain of the commanders a renown extending beyond the sea—a renown which we of the North could not suppress, even if we would. In personal character, also, not a few of the military leaders of the South enforce forbearance; the memory of others the North refrains from disparaging; and some, with more or less of reluctance, she can respect. Posterity, sympathizing with our convictions, but removed from our passions, may perhaps go farther here. If George IV. could, out of the graceful instinct of a gentleman, raise an honorable monument in the great fane of Christendom over the remains of the enemy of his dynasty, Charles Edward, the invader of England and victor in the rout at Preston Pans—upon whose head the king's ancestor but one reign removed had set a price — is it probable that the grandchildren of General Grant will pursue with rancor, or slur by sour neglect, the memory of Stonewall Jackson?

But the South herself is not wanting in recent histories and biographies which record the deeds of her chieftains—writings freely published at the North by loyal houses, widely read here, and with a deep though saddened interest. By students of the war such works are hailed as welcome accessories, and tending to the completeness of the record.

Supposing a happy issue out of present perplexities, then, in the generation next to come, Southerners there will be yielding allegiance to the Union, feeling all their interests bound up in it, and yet cherishing unrebuked that kind of feeling for the memory of the soldiers of the fallen Confederacy that Burns, Scott, and the Ettrick Shepherd felt for. the memory of the gallant clansmen ruined through their fidelity to the Stuarts— a feeling whose passion was tempered by the poetry imbuing it, and which in no wise affected their loyalty to the Georges, and which, it may be added, indirectly contributed excellent things to literature. But, setting this view aside, dishonorable would it be in the South were she willing to abandon to shame the memory of brave men who with signal personal disinterestedness warred in her behalf, though from motives, as we believe, so deplorably astray.

Patriotism is not baseness, neither is it inhumanity. The mourners who this summer bear flowers to the mounds of the Virginian and Georgian dead are, in their domestic bereavement and proud affection, as sacred in the eye of Heaven as are those who go with similar offerings of tender grief and love into the cemeteries of our Northern martyrs. And yet, in one aspect, how needless to point the contrast.

Cherishing such sentiments, it will hardly occasion surprise that, in looking over the battle-pieces in the foregoing collection, I have been tempted to withdraw or modify some of them, fearful lest in presenting, though but dramatically and by way of a poetic record, the passions and epithets of civil war, I might be contributing to a bitterness which every sensible American must wish at an end. So, too, with the emotion of victory as reproduced on some pages, and particularly toward the close. It should not be construed into an exultation misapplied—an exultation as ungenerous as unwise, and made to minister, however indirectly, to that kind of censoriousness too apt to be produced in certain natures by success after trying reverses. Zeal is not of necessity religion, neither is it always of the same essence with poetry or patriotism.

There were excesses which marked the conflict, most of which are perhaps inseparable from a civil strife so intense and prolonged, and involving warfare in some border countries new and imperfectly civilized. Barbarities also there were, for which the Southern people collectively can hardly be held responsible, though perpetrated by ruffians in their name. But surely other qualities — exalted ones — courage and fortitude matchless, were likewise displayed, and largely ; and justly may these be held the characteristic traits, and not the former.

In this view, what Northern writer, however patriotic, but must revolt from acting on paper a part any way akin to that of the live dog to the dead lion ; and yet it is right to rejoice for our triumph, so far as it may justly imply an advance for our whole country and for humanity.

Let it be held no reproach to any one that he pleads for reasonable consideration for our late enemies, now stricken down and unavoidably debarred, for the time, from speaking through authorized agencies for themselves. Nothing has been urged here in the foolish hope of conciliating those men — few in number, we trust—who have resolved never to be reconciled to the

Union. On such hearts every thing is thrown away except it be religious commiseration, and the sincerest. Yet let them call to mind that unhappy Secessionist, not a military man, who with impious alacrity fired the first shot of the Civil War at Sumter, and a little more than four years afterward fired the last one into his own heart at Richmond.

Noble was the gesture into which patriotic passion surprised the people in a utilitarian time and country; yet the glory of the war falls short of its pathos — a pathos which now at last ought to disarm all animosity.

How many and earnest thoughts still rise, and how hard to repress them. We feel what past years have been, and years, unretarded years, shall come. May we all have moderation; may we all show candor. Though, perhaps, nothing could ultimately have averted the strife, and though to treat of human actions is to deal wholly with second causes, nevertheless, let us not cover up or try to extenuate what, humanly speaking, is the truth— namely, that those unfraternal denunciations, continued through years, and which at last inflamed to deeds that ended in bloodshed, were reciprocal; and that, had the preponderating strength and the prospect of its unlim- ited increase lain on the other side, on ours might have lain those actions which now in our late opponents we stigmatize under the name of Rebellion. As frankly

M

let us own — what it would be unbecoming to parade were foreigners concerned — that our triumph was won not more by skill and bravery than by superior resources and crushing numbers; that it was a triumph, too, over a people for years politically misled by designing men, and also by some honestly-erring men, who from their position could not have been otherwise than broadly influential; a people who, though, indeed, they sought to perpetuate the curse of slavery, and even extend it, were not the authors of it, but (less fortunate, not less righteous than we) were the fated inheritors; a people who, having a like origin with ourselves, share essentially in whatever worthy qualities we may possess. No one can add to the lasting reproach which hopeless defeat has now cast upon Secession by withholding the recognition of these verities.

Surely we ought to take it to heart that that kind of pacification, based upon principles operating equally all over the land, which lovers of their country yearn for, and which our arms, though signally triumphant, did not bring about, and which law-making, however anxious, or energetic, or repressive, never by itself can achieve, may yet be largely aided by generosity of sentiment public and private. Some revisionary legislation and adaptive is indispensable; but with this should harmoniously work another kind of prudence, not unallied with entire magnanimity. Benevolence and policy — Christianity and Machiavelli — dissuade from penal severities toward the subdued. Abstinence here is as obligatory as considerate care for our unfortunate fellow-men late in bonds, and, if observed, would equally prove to be wise forecast. The great qualities of the South, those attested in the War, we can perilously alienate, or we may make them nationally available at need.

The blacks, in their infant pupilage to freedom, appeal to the sympathies of every humane mind. The paternal guardianship which for the interval government exercises over them was prompted equally by duty and benevolence. Yet such kindliness should not be allowed to exclude kindliness to communities who stand nearer to us in nature. For the future of the freed slaves we may well be concerned; but the future of the whole country, involving the future of the blacks, urges a paramount claim upon our anxiety. Effective benignity, like the Nile, is not narrow in its bounty, and true policy is always broad. To be sure, it is vain to seek to glide, with moulded words, over the difficulties of the situation. And for them who are neither partisans, nor enthusiasts, nor theorists, nor cynics, there are some doubts not readily to be solved. And there are fears. Why is not the cessation of war now at length attended with the settled calm of peace?

Wherefore in a clear sky do we still turn our eyes toward the South, as the Neapolitan, months after the eruption, turns his toward Vesuvius? Do we dread lest the repose may be deceptive? In the recent convulsion has the crater but shifted? Let us revere that sacred uncertainty which forever impends over men and nations. Those of us who always abhorred slavery as an atheistical iniquity, gladly we join in the exulting chorus of humanity over its downfall. But we should remember that emancipation was accomplished not by deliberate legislation; only through agonized violence could so mighty a result be effected. In our natural solicitude to confirm the benefit of liberty to the blacks, let us forbear from measures of dubious constitutional rightfulness toward our white countrymen — measures of a nature to provoke, among other of the last evils, exterminating hatred of race toward race. In imagination let us place ourselves in the unprecedented position of the Southerners — their position as regards the millions of ignorant manumitted slaves in their midst, for whom some of us now claim the suffrage. Let us be Christians toward our fellow-whites, as well as philanthropists toward the blacks, our fellow-men. In all things, and toward all, we are enjoined to do as we would be done by. Nor should we forget that benevolent desires, after passing a certain point, can not undertake their own fulfillment without incurring the risk of evils beyond those sought to be remedied. Something may well be left to the graduated care of future legislation, and to heaven. In one point of view the co-existence of the two races in the South — whether the negro be bond or free—seems (even as it did to Abraham Lincoln) a grave evil. Emancipation has ridded the country of the reproach, but not wholly of the calamity. Especially in the present transition period for both races in the South, more or less of trouble may not unreasonably be anticipated ; but let us not hereafter be too swift to charge the blame exclusively in any one quarter. With certain evils men must be more or less patient. Our institutions have a potent digestion, and may in time convert and assimilate to good all elements thrown in, however originally alien.

But, so far as immediate measures looking toward permanent Re-establishment are concerned, no consideration should tempt us to pervert the national victory into oppression for the vanquished. Should plausible promise of eventual good, or a deceptive or spurious sense of duty, lead us to essay this, count we must on serious consequences, not the least of which would be divisions among the Northern adherents of the Union. Assuredly, if any honest Catos there be who thus far have gone with us, no longer will they do so, but oppose us, and as resolutely as hitherto they have supported. But this path of thought leads toward those waters of bitterness from which one can only turn aside and be silent.

But supposing Re-establishment so far advanced that the Southern seats in Congress are occupied, and by men qualified in accordance with those cardinal principles of representative government which hitherto have prevailed in the land—what then? Why, the Congressmen elected by the people of the South will—represent the people of the South. This may seem a flat conclusion; but, in view of the last five years, may there not be latent significance in it? What will be the temper of those Southern members? and, confronted by them, what will be the mood of our own representatives? In private life true reconciliation seldom follows a violent quarrel; but, if subsequent intercourse be unavoidable, nice observances and mutual are indispensable to the prevention of a new rupture. Amity itself can only be maintained by reciprocal respect, and true friends are punctilious equals. On the floor of Congress North and South are to come together after a passionate duel, in which the South, though proving her valor, has been made to bite the dust. Upon differences in debate shall acrimonious recriminations be exchanged? shall censorious superiority assumed by one section provoke defiant self-assertion on the other? shall

Manassas and Chickamauga be retorted for Chattanooga
and Richmond? Under the supposition that the full
Congress will be composed of gentlemen, all this is im-
possible. Yet, if otherwise, it needs no prophet of Is-
rael to foretell the end. The maintenance of Congres-
sional decency in the future will rest mainly with the
North. Rightly will more forbearance be required from
the North than the South, for the North is victor.

But some there are who may deem these latter thoughts
inapplicable, and for this reason : Since the test-oath
operatively excludes from Congress all who in any way
participated in Secession, therefore none but Southern-
ers wholly in harmony with the North are eligible to
seats. This is true for the time being. But the oath
is alterable ; and in the wonted fluctuations of parties
not improbably it will undergo alteration, assuming such
a form, perhaps, as not to bar the admission into the
National Legislature of men who represent the pop-
ulations lately in revolt. Such a result would involve
no violation of the principles of democratic government.
Not readily can one perceive how the political existence
of the millions of late Secessionists can permanently be
ignored by this Republic. The years of the war tried
our devotion to the Union ; the time of peace may test
the sincerity of our faith in democracy.

In no spirit of opposition, not by way of challenge,

is any thing here thrown out. These thoughts are sincere ones; they seem natural—inevitable. Here and there they must have suggested themselves to many thoughtful patriots. And, if they be just thoughts, ere long they must have that weight with the public which already they have had with individuals.

For that heroic band—those children of the furnace who, in regions like Texas and Tennessee, maintained their fidelity through terrible trials—we of the North felt for them, and profoundly we honor them. Yet passionate sympathy, with resentments so close as to be almost domestic in their bitterness, would hardly in the present juncture tend to discreet legislation. Were the Unionists and Secessionists but as Guelphs and Ghibellines? If not, then far be it from a great nation now to act in the spirit that animated a triumphant town-faction in the Middle Ages. But crowding thoughts must at last be checked; and, in times like the present, one who desires to be impartially just in the expression of his views, moves as among sword-points presented on every side.

Let us pray that the terrible historic tragedy of our time may not have been enacted without instructing our whole beloved country through terror and pity; and may fulfillment verify in the end those expectations which kindle the bards of Progress and Humanity.

THE END.